MW00535323

Bible Interpretations

Seventh Series

January 1 – March 31, 1893

Ezra, Zechariah, Nehemiah, Esther, Proverbs

Bible Interpretations

Seventh Series

Ezra, Zechariah, Nehemiah, Esther, Proverbs

These Bible Interpretations were given during the early eighteen nineties at the Christian Science Theological Seminary at Chicago, Illinois. This Seminary was independent of the First Church of Christ Scientist in Boston, Mass.

By

Emma Curtis Hopkins

President of the Christian Science Theological Seminary at Chicago, Illinois

WISEWOMAN PRESS

Bible Interpretations: Seventh Series

By Emma Curtis Hopkins

© WiseWoman Press

Managing Editor: Michael Terranova

ISBN: 978-0-945385-57-8

WiseWoman Press

Vancouver, WA 98665

www.wisewomanpress.com

www.emmacurtishopkins.com

CONTENTS

Editors Note

All lessons starting with the Seventh Series of Bible Interpretations will be Sunday postings from the Inter-Ocean Newspaper in Chicago, Illinois. Many of the lessons in the following series were retrieved from the International New Thought Association Archives, in Mesa, Arizona by, Rev Joanna Rogers. Many others were retrieved from libraries in Chicago, and the Library of Congress, by Rev. Natalie Jean.

All the lessons follow the Sunday School Lesson Plan published in "Peloubet's International Sunday School Lessons". The passages to be studied are selected by an International Committee of traditional Bible Scholars.

Some of the Emma's lessons don't have a title. In these cases the heading will say "Comments and Explanations of the Golden Text," followed by the Bible passages to be studied.

Foreword

By Rev. Natalie R. Jean

I have read many teachings by Emma Curtis Hopkins, but the teachings that touch the very essence of my soul are her Bible Interpretations. There are many books written on the teachings of the Bible, but none can touch the surface of the true messages more than these Bible interpretations. With each word you can feel and see how Spirit spoke through Emma. The mystical interpretations take you on a wonderful journey to Self Realization.

Each passage opens your consciousness to a new awareness of the realities of life. The illusions of life seem to disappear through each interpretation. Emma teaches that we are the key that unlocks the doorway to the light that shines within. She incorporates ideals of other religions into her teachings, in order to understand the commonalities, so that there is a complete understanding of our Oneness. Emma opens our eyes and mind to a better today and exciting future.

Emma Curtis Hopkins, one of the Founders of New Thought teaches us to love ourselves, to speak our Truth, and to focus on our Good. My life has moved in wonderful directions because of her teachings. I know the only thing that can move me in this world is God. May these interpretations guide you to a similar path and may you truly remember that "There Is Good For You and You Ought to Have It."

Introduction

Emma Curtis Hopkins was born in 1849 in Killingsly, Connecticut. She passed on April 8, 1925. Mrs. Hopkins had a marvelous education and could read many of the worlds classical texts in their original language. During her extensive studies she was always able to discover the Universal Truths in each of the world's sacred traditions. She quotes from many of these teachings in her writings. As she was a very private person, we know little about her personal life. What we do know has been gleaned from other people or from the archived writings we have been able to discover.

Emma Curtis Hopkins was one of the greatest influences on the New Thought movement in the United States. She taught over 50,000 people the Universal Truth of knowing "God is All there is." She taught many of founders of early New Thought, and in turn these individuals expanded the influence of her teachings. All of her writings encourage the student to enter into a personal relationship with God. She presses us to deny anything except the Truth of this spiritual Presence in every area of our lives. This is the central focus of all her teachings.

The first six series of Bible Interpretations were presented at her seminary in Chicago, Illinois. The remaining Series', probably close to thirty, were printed in the Inter Ocean Newspaper in Chicago. Many of the lessons are no longer available for various reasons. It is the intention of WiseWoman Press to publish as many of these Bible Interpretations as possible. Our hope is that any missing lessons will be found or directed to us.

I am very honored to join the long line of people that have been involved in publishing Emma Curtis Hopkins's Bible Interpretations. Some confusion exists as to the numbering sequence of the lessons. In the early 1920's many of the lessons were published by the Highwatch Fellowship. Inadvertently the first two lessons were omitted from the numbering system. Rev. Joanna Rogers has corrected this mistake by finding the first two lessons and restoring them to their rightful place in the order. Rev. Rogers has been able to find many of the missing lessons at the International New Thought Alliance archives in Mesa, Arizona. Rev. Rogers painstakingly scoured the archives for the missing lessons as well as for Mrs. Hopkins other works. She has published much of what was discovered. WiseWoman Press is now publishing the correctly numbered series of the Bible Interpretations.

In the early 1940's, there was a resurgence of interest in Emma's works. At that time, Highwatch Fellowship began to publish many of her writings, and it was then that *High Mysticism,* her seminal work was published. Previously, the material contained in High Mysticism was only available as individual lessons and was brought together in book form for the first time. Although there were many errors in these first publications and many Bible verses were incorrectly quoted, I am happy to announce that WiseWoman Press is now publishing *High Mysticism* in the a corrected format. This corrected form was scanned faithfully from the original, individual lessons.

The next person to publish some of the Bible Lessons was Rev. Marge Flotron from the Ministry of Truth International in Chicago, Illinois. She published the Bible Lessons as well as many of Emma's other works. By her initiative, Emma's writings were brought to a larger audience when DeVorss & Company, a longtime publisher of Truth Teachings, took on the publication of her key works.

In addition, Dr. Carmelita Trowbridge, founding minister of The Sanctuary of Truth in Alhambra, California, inspired her assistant minister, Rev. Shirley Lawrence, to publish many of Emma's works, including the first three series of Bible Interpretations. Rev. Lawrence created mail order courses for many of these Series. She has graciously passed on any information she had, in order to assure that these works continue to inspire individuals and groups who are called to further study of the teachings of Mrs. Hopkins.

Finally, a very special acknowledgement goes to Rev Natalie Jean, who has worked diligently to retrieve several of Emma's lessons from the Library of Congress, as well as libraries in Chicago. Rev. Jean hand-typed many of the lessons she found on microfilm. Much of what she found is on her website, www.highwatch.net.

It is with a grateful heart that I am able to pass on these wonderful teachings. I have been studying dear Emma's works for fifteen years. I was introduced to her writings by my mentor and teacher, Rev. Marcia Sutton. I have been overjoyed with the results of delving deeply into these Truth Teachings.

In 2004, I wrote a Sacred Covenant entitled "Resurrecting Emma," and created a website, www.emmacurtishopkins.com. The result of creating this covenant and website has brought many of Emma's works into my hands and has deepened my faith in God. As a result of my love for these works, I was led to become a member of Wise-Woman Press and to publish these wonderful teachings. God is Good.

My understanding of Truth from these divinely inspired teachings keeps bringing great Joy, Freedom, and Peace to my life.

Dear reader; It is with an open heart that I offer these works to you, and I know they will touch you as they have touched me. Together we are living in the Truth that God is truly present, and living for and through each of us.

The greatest Truth Emma presented to us is "My Good is my God, Omnipresent, Omnipotent and Omniscient."

Rev. Michael Terranova

WiseWoman Press

Vancouver, Washington, 2010

LESSON I

ALL IS AS ALLAH WILLS

Ezra 1

Khaled Knew that he was of The Genii

"Khaled" knew that he was of the genii, and the genii knew that all is as Allah wills. Mortal forces might struggle and strive against him, but he rested in the formula, "There is no Allah, but Allah." When all the wise men and powerful ones of the realm thought it cowardice not to stand forth and defend his reputation, he would say over the formula, "There is no power but Allah." And so all nature roused herself to move victory in his pathway.

He defeated every adversity by a spiritual way, not by the power of material advantages. There come days when it is well to ponder where we stand and what we believe. Do we believe that it is the intention of our God to give us our life and we nothing for our life? Do we believe that it is the intention of God for us that we have our health and we do nothing for our health?

A certain faith cure advocate noticed that while she was being healed by the power of faith, if she undertook to eat or drink or walk thinking that these would accelerate her recovery she fell back instead of progressing. She might eat, drink, and walk all she pleased, so she did not have as a reason for doing that such practices would help heal her. She had to be true to the principle she had espoused.

So that by agreeing that God has charge of our life, and we will do nothing for our life, no visible change in our modes of notion might take place, yet the *raison d'etre*, the reason why we should do thus or so would be supremely different.

Certain men arise who call themselves Jesus Christ come again. They do not mean that their spiritual nature only is Jesus Christ, on the principle of "Jesus Christ in you the hope of glory," but that they, *in toto*, as they appear, coarse flesh and all, are Jesus Christ. Their talk sounds very like those others who say that God, the universal spirit, is one in substance, nature, and word with their Spirit, therefore they and God are one, but the idea lying back of their words is infinitely different.

There is practical demonstration in marvelous protection from disease, accident, death, diversity, by the acknowledgment of spirit as God whether we think of spirit as the soul of the rock of our own

2

life. The very acknowledgment is sure to demonstrate.

It is written in a story called "The Year Ten Thousand," that we then make the tour of the globe in twenty-four hours by ascending into the atmosphere above the attraction of gravitation and there waiting for the planet to turn over once. We then alight wheresoever we please on the then much civilized earth.

<u>The Spring of Love</u>

All these ideas touch that spring of love of freedom from trammels, which we all have in our nature. And we all have the love of freedom from entangling human limitations because freedom is our birthright. Whoever brings us the teaching that sets us free from our heathen conditions is enacting the role of Cyrus to the Jews, as recorded in this lesson (Ezra, first chapter). There is a hard way of being set free from sickness and disease. It is by the way of nauseous potions, difficult exercises, and knives of modern doctoring. This is Babylon's way. Whoever gets tangled in its methods is in bondage to the heathen." For the wisdom of the schools is foolishness with God."

There is a way of being set free from disease and sickness by getting above and out of the range of the attracting gravitations of teachings and utterly letting go expectation of assistance from material prescriptions. Let me be written on the pages of human history as one who defeated disease and sickness by the way of the spirit only, unaided by mortal remedies.

There is a way of being provided for and protected by the hard and laborious processes of barrier (from Barrier Treaty, during 18th Century) and deal, commerce, mechanics, shrewd manipulations of men and events, watchings of material combinations. Those who succeed by the highest arts possible to these processes are not able to teach their methods to the millions, so that they are one step ahead in peace of mind than they were before the successful operators began.

There is a way of being provided for and protected by listening to spiritual teachings. It is sure to lift the swarming millions into peace, where "They shall forget misery as waters that pass away." Let me be written on the pages of human history as one who defeated adversity by the way of the spirit only, unaided by any process recommended or practiced by artisan, financier of materiality.

The prophecy reads that when one has utterly defeated ignorance, disease, death, poverty, by spiritual understanding alone, he shall be able to tell his way to the whole world. But Rothschild, Gould, Cleveland, can not teach the millions by what subtle intricacy of skill or effort they wrought out success.

If the way of Jesus Christ taught was listened to all the world would speedily lift up its free head. But if the way of these men were listened to and practiced faithfully; it would not work with any or for any but themselves. *"Come unto me all ye that labor and are heavy laden, and I will give you rest,"* (Matthew 11:28). Let me give all my time and talent, energy and docility to learning the Jesus Christ way of prosperity for every creature by my prosperity, intelligence for every creature by my intelligence, health for every creature by my intelligence which I can not (help bestowing if I learn his way.

The Coming of Jesus

Cyrus prefigured the coming of Jesus. Cyrus king of the Persian Empire, 558 B.C., gave all the Jews who would receive it, their liberty to arise and go from captivity in Babylon to freedom in Jerusalem. Jesus, A.D. 30, gave all the earth of who would receive it liberty from sickness, poverty, death.

As a spiritual doctrine of the highest order there is now offered to all who will understand it, freedom from even the memories of disease, poverty, death.

The world had wrought out by bloodshed and forced labor great successes according to its way of thinking while the Jews were in captivity. The King had by these means built Babylon into a magnificence of architecture beyond record. Rome was preparing for a republic. The great public library at Athens was opened. Pythagoras and the new multiplication table astonished the learned.

Solon and *Jesop* and Confucius were shedding abroad the mental quickening of their genius.

Cyrus the Zoroastrian set the Jewish captives free. They had got into ruts. They had stiffened into worshipers of forms and formulas. The meanings of the forms and formulas were bottled close. Cyrus, the believer in the doctrine of one supreme God, The Good, the life and light of all things, Ormuzd, Lord and God of all, set the captives free.

So when Jesus came, He opened up to the worshipers of existing forms the wells of their inner meanings.

> *"Call no man upon earth your father, for One is your father."*
>
> *"Do not think that I will accuse you."*
>
> *"All things that I have heard from the Father I have told you."*
>
> *"All power is given unto me."*
>
> *"Where I am there may ye be also."*

He was a Zoroastrian in his teachings of universal freedom. All who received the liberty He offered could work miracles to show their independence of death, disease, poverty, ignorance, when they listened to the spacious arguments of materiality they became again entangled and demonstrations ceased.

It is the Zoroastrian doctrine that again blows the fresh winds through stiffened formality of the undemonstrating formulas of this age. Architec-

6

ture, scholasticism, pollution, and mechanics are at their height. Religion was boundless territory and scentless treasure, yet the captive exiles from prosperity were never further from home.

"The Lord of Life and Light is One." The Lord of health and prosperity is One. Whithersoever we flee there waiteth the Spirit of help. Into whatsoever task, we entangle ourselves led wither by the spacious gravitations of to-day's high skill in mortal methods, still above us and around us woos the spiritual breath, able to cut the cords that bind us, without our struggling to set us free. We have only to accept the offer.

"Then rose up the chief of the fathers of Judah and Benjamin to build the house of the Lord at Jerusalem." When there shall be the rising up to build the house, where there shall be no teaching of a God, who lets His people go hungry, cold, sick, to test their quality, nor leaves countless millions languishing in savagery waiting for the sciences of materiality to redeem, then see how the radiance of that lighthouse shall breathe the knowledge of their own relation to the surrounding spirit to the whole globe full, to the twinkling of an eye.

He who tries for the prosperity that belongs to him by the processes that have been practiced for ages has not received the prosperity that was born into life from the beginning for him, though he has a great name and many millions, for who is set free from these processes has a prosperity which

7

he giveth to all the earth, each creature in equal share.

He whose health and strength and beauty and wisdom are found by the spiritual teaching can bring health, strength, wisdom, and loveliness to all living things. By these signs we may know when Cyrus and Jesus the Zoroastrians are here to this age.

Inter-Ocean Newspaper, January 1, 1893

LESSON II

ZERUBBABEL'S HIGH IDEAL

Ezra 2:8-13

A Temple Which Shall Stand for The Highest Doctrine.

The Silence of the Idealist the Power Of Omnipotence.

The True Principle.

Cyrus, the Persian, worshiped Ormuzd. Doubtless he had heard the priests of his religion chanting many times the invocation: "I invoke and celebrate Ahuramazda, brilliant, greatest. He thinks good, and to those who think evil he is not known. He speaks good, and to those who speak evil he does not belong. He does good, and to those who do evil he does not belong."

This formula held by any mind concerning Deity will give large toleration and great kindness. It had made Cyrus clear minded enough to see the points of resemblance between Ormuzd and Jeho-

9

vah. Daniel had shown him the prophecies of a new temple being built about that time in which to worship the true God. He felt that he was the chosen superintendent of that building.

Fulfillments of Prophecies

The feeling that one's work is fulfilling, literally some devout prophecy has the effect of angels coming and ministering unto us. Jesus Christ would often say, "That the Scripture might be fulfilled;" "thus it is written." Outside of the zeal inspired by confidence in the divinity of Daniel's books, Cyrus had no call to build a temple to Jehovah, but the beauty of the best Zoroastrians was that they were not bigoted. Jesus was a Zoroastrian in that he called duty, love, spirit, light, universal good, knowing no evil. To the bigoted feeling so often encountered among his people this was blasphemous.

Here we read that certain of the old men howled when the foundation of the new house of Jehovah was finished because it was not built by a Solomon. There has never been a church or temple or school built on the true principle yet. A church or temple founded to proclaim that God is omnipresent would necessitate the preachers saying, "There is only God." This would be so at variance with the sight of the eyes and the hearing of the ears that unless they were "God intoxicated," like Spinoza, they could not tell such a thing. A school founded on the right principle must be founded to proclaim that Divine Wisdom is omnipresent. This would necessitate the teachers saying that they were always standing in the presence of Omniscience and speaking to Omniscience. Here again the sight of their eyes and hearing of their ears would dispute them unless they were touched by the heavenly fire of the quickening truth they would feel guilty to take their religion so literally.

But there will be such a church and school founded one day. The healing love of the true God therein proclaimed shall cause all who step over the threshold to be instantly cured of all their maladies. There shall be beauty for ashes to the broken in life. There shall be the oil of joy for mourning. There shall be instantaneous straightening of the deformities. There shall be sudden wisdom gleam over the faces and think through the mind of the foolish. All these conditions having resulted from belief in some character of Orzmud, Jehovah, which he does not possess, belief in some conduct he is incapable of exercising, belief in his absence and unwillingness, where the belief is removed the conditions will fall.

Do you suppose if your mind were trained in music so that you could compose symphonies, sonatas, requiems, far beyond the uncompanioned genius Beethoven, Mozart, Mendelssohn, that the light of your high mentality would be a healing radiance wherever you should walk, so that the rays of your thought quality would cure paralysis, spinal curvature, idiocy? No, you would more likely make everybody uneasy and restless by the discord of difference between their mental trend and your own.

Do you suppose that if you were so skillful with your fingers that you could perform the delicate operation of tracheotomy and it would make your mental presence a cure for diphtheria? No; a Boston paper tells us that though so many are marvelously skillful in medicine and surgery that malady is more skillfully handled in its cases than the greatest of them.

The Great Physician

But at the first trump of the teaching of Jesus, disease flees away. At the very mention of His name many a malady has disappeared like as the shadow of a post at noonday.

It is related of one man that, being terribly injured, his surgeons said he could not live till morning. He then began to whisper the name Jesus Christ. He used all the strength and force he had left in him to repeat the name. Soon he could speak it aloud. After a while he could shout it. He did not allow himself to think of anything else. Nothing diverted his attention. They thought he was crazy, but in the morning he was well.

"In My name heal the sick."

If a great and learned man asks for more surgeons' tools and a greater number of pills and bottles we promptly give him our millions to buy them with. But these appliances and compositions are not according to the orders of Jesus Christ: "In My name."

There were 50,000 who took to the journey from Babylon to Jerusalem. They found Jerusalem in ruins as it had been for fifty years, since its complete destruction by Nebuchadnezzar. On every side the heathen had so mixed their ideas with the peasant Israelites that there in that city, where it was meet that the temple should be built, there was no clear understanding of the high, pure doctrine, which the men of Daniel's type represented. These refused to unite or coalesce with the compromising practices and ideas of the half-and-half people in Jerusalem.

By not uniting with them because they did not represent the principles for which the temples should stand the exiles from Babylon have been greatly blamed, for it delayed the building of the temple fourteen years. But when a temple is founded to one principle its representatives must stand to that principle. As high as the Israelites could speak of what they believe so high must the temple people believe.

History repeats itself. The last temple shall stand for the highest doctrine ever preached. And the highest doctrine is that there is only God. In God there is nothing to fear. We, therefore, being in God, fear nothing. Hunger and sickness, cold and death do not abide in God. We abide in God; therefore these abide not in us.

13

Followers of the Light

It is here in this third chapter of Ezra is told that "Zerubbabel, the son of Shealtiel," set forward the work of the house of the Lord. This name means, "born in Babylon." There are certain minds, which were brought up in the very heart of intellectual training, money getting manufacturing, religious formality. Nevertheless, when they hear the principles of Orzmud, the Lord of Life and light universal proclaimed, they cannot help following those principles in their reasonings, wither so ever they lead. Away from the teachings of their books they turn, led on by the light of a doctrine they have never seen anybody trust absolutely. On out of sight of the home of their youth they follow where the light beckons, it is their duty to follow.

Away down into Jerusalem where their heavenly ideals are taken and adulterated with individual opinions, still they keep the star of their confidence in sight. These are "Zerubbabels." For them the house of the Lord arises in Jerusalem. And there shall be shouting of joy because of the temple, exactly as when the Zerubbabel, in this lesson, laid the foundations of a house, the right description of God they had made.

History records that the house was delayed because the enemies of the idealist Zerubbabel circulated slanderous reports concerning him. But the delay counted for nothing. Time is nothing to principle. It always comes off victorious any way.

The enemies of the mighty principle always get broken where they pit themselves against it. There is the will that will be done. If we have a will that is supposed to, with that will we have some unyielding hardship of sickness to represent our opposition. The instant we yield, the hardship is gone. *"Thy will, not mine be done,"* says Jesus, whether he saw how much he was opposed to the way things were going if he brought any of the traditions of his bringing up to bear in the situation.

How silent Zerubbabel was, he was born in Babylon and those heart-stricken pulled him hither, but whose star held him fixed in Jerusalem! The idealist has to be silent. His motives are not apprehensible; those who have nothing like them. But the silence is the power of omnipotence; his central being is continually lighted as his health and the fountains of the fires of good beyond God. Each day his ideals are clearer. Each hour his thoughts gather enough force to heal and revive the drooping world with.

The idealist of today has the life of Jesus to remind him, what can be done by holding fast by the doctrine of light and life in the highest.

Doctrine of Spinoza

"I choose to know spirit rather than imagine matter," said Spinoza, "I choose to believe that if I keep my mind on the words of Jesus Christ concerning my life, I need not try to save my life; it will be loved by the spirit of life forever more. I choose to believe that my health and strength are eternal. I choose to believe that my breath and home shall come straight from spirit without any struggle of mine."

As the idealist of this hour, as high as Zerubbabel cast his lot, so much demonstration of God did he make. As high as Spinoza has his faith, so much demonstration of spirit did he receive. As high the idealist of this hour plans his hopes, so much demonstration of the watch care of God, will he receive. *"Bread shall be given him; his waters always be sure. His place of defense shall be ammunitions of rocks." "He shall be delivered in six troubles, yea, in seven; there shall no evil touch him."*

Where the idealist abides, whose expectations are set on the coming of God with the cure of my people, there the people shall be well. Where the idealist walks, whose head is fixed above, there the angels feed and clothe by moving down on the possessions hidden for ages to open them for the demonstration of the miracles of the new age.

Inter-Ocean Newspaper, January 8, 1893

LESSON III

DIVINE RAYS OF POWER

Ezra 4

Conscious and Unconscious Wonders of Mightiness

The Twelve Lessons of Science of Zerubbabel and His High Ideas

In a great theater in a foreign country, when the star actress is absent and her place is taken by somebody whose genius in playing the part transcends her own, her steadfast admirers hisses the playing of the substitute. If the young genius is not crushed by such treatment, she finally makes her way.

Genius is a fire, which flames from Divinity. And Divinity is omnipotent. The beauty of every life is that it has some one gate leading outward from the inner fires of God to the world in which we walk. To let that gate stand open is to see all the obstacles of the human experience melt before you. Nothing can resist genius. The way most of

17

the world has been acted with its own Divine flame has been to flinch and cringe when it has been spoken slightingly to, or else work along the hardest lines it could devise to bring out its successes.

All flinching and cringing when you have been spoken slightingly of, or found fault with, is simply the love of approbation exhibiting itself. At such times if you will fall back on the knowledge that there is one shining strength that moment putting itself forward from you, which they cannot damage with fear or grief, you will feel the support of that invisible fire. There is only a ray of unchangeable delight going forth from you, which nobody can hurt. Just know this fact when failure, misfortune, unkindness confront you. Simply knowing it, will cause it to shine with hotter and hotter intensity, till your birthright of mastery of the universe is wholly secured to you.

Zerubbabel, of this lesson was the idealist of his age. He was one who had this secret of falling back on the one flame that never is wanting from any character. He was of a nature to feel hurt and astonished that those he expected to see his ideals were proposing to use him just long enough to set themselves up as leaders of a work along his line instead of their own line. It was his only weapon of defense that was taken by them as being for personal honors, while he was honestly carrying out a great principle regardless of personal aggrandizement, that he kept still and watched his one ray of power.

If you can not see that you have any ray of power, take the *ipse dixit*;(He Himself said) it is so. Have one stream of mightiness, which nothing ever dismays or hurts. Keep still and think about it when you are misused, as Zerubbabel of Haggai, second, is described as being. Soon you will rise with the splendid victory of this triumphant idealist, who was bound as a signet upon the arm of Jehovah for keeping still when misused and waiting for his ray of might to win his cause. He waited fifteen years. That was because he did not know the science of his own conduct. If he had known why he instinctively kept still, why he kept right on working a cause whose exponents, with only a handful of exceptions misused him, he would have built a wonderful temple before. You, knowing the science of your conduct, the reasons why you keep still will find your ray of mightiness and indestructible genius working much more rapidly.

The first step toward victory is to know you have one ray of genius. The second step is to believe that the one ray was born with you to take care of you. The conduct you carry on is silent confidence as your weapon of defense. The beauty of its goodness is that it does not want you to do anything whatsoever only to know it is going forth from you. If you know it is streaming out from you, you can not help loving it. Then you do not quarrel with your adversaries. Quarreling, answering, trying other ways to defend yourself from people's misuse, is like David's attempting fight in Saul's armor. Your ray of Divine Fire is quite enough for your entire defense.

Haggai, the prophet, comforted Zerubbabel with promises of the greatness of his temple he was preparing to build to represent the idealistic teaching concerning God. You will be surprised to find how many people there are in the world 'with prophetic feelings for the encouragement of those who are inclined to trust their genius. Whether you are scientifically conscious of why you are leaning on your ideas or not you will be prophesied unto. Haggai came to Zerubbabel with the most enchanting promises. Hear this one: *"Be strong, O Zerubbabel for I am with you, saith the Lord, my spirit remaineth with you, I will shake the nations and the desire of all nations shall come; and will fill this house with glory. The silver is mine and the gold is mine, saith the Lord of Hosts. The glory of this latter house shall be greater than of the former, and in this place will I give peace. '*

There is a prophecy of the same kind relating to the new house to come forth where the whole teaching is to be, that the silver and gold of the planet are amenable to this Divine ray. Whoever lies back on it will find his silver and gold coming to him easily. He will find his paths all laid out for him before hand. The storm and stress of energetic action are not legitimate. They are not Jesus Christ.

By the old hazards men have built wonderful steamers, magnificent public buildings. By the travail of effort the cities of the world stand in their splendor. Their glory is great and the pride men take in civilization is puffed up within them, but the cities that are to arise by the working efficiency of confidence in the divine ray of each man, woman and child, as it is to be taught in the new temple, will not have any horrors of bloodshed, peril by sea or land, the enriched and the beggared, the overworked and the under paid, lying back of their splendors.

The rich and powerful refused to help the idealist Zerubbabel. His own colleagues maligned him, but his radiance burned down all disadvantages. We shall not wait fourteen or fifteen years to build the latter temple for we have science of spirit. Jesus Christ had the Conscious Knowledge of the way he performed all his miracles. Conscious Knowledge of the why and wherefores is science. By a very little exact reasoning, from promise to as high as you are willing to go in reasoning, you will become very conscious of your processes. Zerubbabel was not conscious. He was simply an astonished silent child. Jesus Christ was conscious.

If your silent presence heals the rheumatism of your neighbor while you are entirely unaware that you are accomplishing it, you are after the unconscious order of Zerubbabel mightiness. If you know in an instant that virtue is going forth from you

like a ray of light, you are of the Jesus Christ order of mightiness. Both ways work, but the
conscious knowledge of what you are about works
more speedily and is something you can always
count on.

The Twelve Lessons of Science

The twelve lessons of science bring out the line
of your genius and teach you to see it work. It will
heal sickness when you realize that in the presence of great sickness that ray of your being does
not believe in sickness, it will bring you silver and
gold for your support when you realize that the
one ray of your being does not believe in want. It
will cure the poverty of your neighbors exactly as
it will cure their diseases. You might want to practice thinking about that one stream of living fire
which is undaunted and fearless streaming forth
from you forever. Just thinking about it will
strengthen your confidence in its power. It is from
knowing the nature and operation of that one with
fire that the Christian Scientists of this hour are
able to tell that their only subsistence is spirit. For
this ray is spiritual, not carnal. They tell that
their only reality is spirit. For it is the only reality
of any of us. All the rest is carnal and unreliable
dreaming.

This stream, being believed in, will take entire
possession of our affairs. Its perpetual command to
the rest of our body and mind is, "Be still and
know that I am God." For it is our God. When certain ones have felt that nature rising strongly,

22

they have spoken aloud for it, saying audibly, "I am God." But the world said they were blasphemous. So they were silent like Zerubbabel. Jesus Christ was not silent, because he knew enough to speak from that nature always. He did not mind the speech of the world.

Inter-Ocean Newspaper, January 15, 1898

LESSON IV

VISIONS OF ZECHARIAH

Zechariah 3

Accuracy with Respect to Deity On Eternal Substance Evil Thoughts Have No Carrying Potency Unaided by Outward Efforts

When a canon-ball tore up the tough ground at Sevastopol a clear spring of water rose up for thirsty soldiers. When the wind blows hard from the land over the sea and then suddenly subsides, the waves come rushing back and inundate the dry soils. When the mind is rent by fierce emotion the clear spring of some new wisdom is uncovered. When the mind is long urged to severe tasks, complete rests brings the powers surging back over the dry dejections of weariness. Zechariah had been agonizing his mind over the depressing circumstances of the returned Jews in Jerusalem. Nothing seemed possible of fulfillment of all the rich promises of Isaiah and Ezekiel. Suddenly in a pause of grief, when it seemed he could not offer any further petitions, for his heart was broken within him, a series if beautiful visions, prophetic of the coming dominion of the spiritual teachings of the Jews, spread before him.

Subconscious Belief in Evil

This lesson takes up the fourth of those visions (see Zech.3). In this vision Joshua is the representative not only of the whole priesthood but also of the entire nation. He stands in Zechariah's vision *"in the presence of an angel of the Lord and Satan standing at the right hand to resist him."* This signifies that the nation has come to a time when the words of good it has thought meet face to face the words of error. Satan is always the representative of the subconscious belief in evil in which religious minded of the world keep hidden deeply within their thoughts. Did you ever know a minister who did not keep it running through his mind that he hoped the Lord would not put upon him such severe trials as he had put upon others? This hope is Satan. It is the insinuation against the mercy and impartial tenderness of Omnipotent Love. It tries to masquerade as gratitude, but that is its subtlety. It is Satan.

When Satan gets ready to externalize in afflictions great moralizers call it dispensations of God. Satan comes out just on time with the "angel of the Lord." The angel of the Lord is beautiful truth, which all religious people think. There are certain affirmations of Deity, which they all make in common. They think they are true. As ideas break forth into conditions the divine affirmations of the religious minded break forth into blessings. One affirmations of Truth which they make, is that God is good and creates the good. They then affirm that He made Satan. Right here, if the religious mind does not deny that God made Satan, it must face up its neglect in the loss of some blessing.

Joshua, representing Israel, stands between the two, Satan and the angel. The angel tells his servants to take away the filthy garments with which Joshua is clothed and put upon him a change of garment. When Israel had gotten exceedingly barren and desolate her past worships should come flowing over her their fruiting time.

No matter how miserably mistaken a mind may be in the nine points, if it has one point in which it is accurate, that accurate point will outwear all the others. Accuracy with respect to Deity is an eternal substance. Errors are made of temporary and insubstantial stuff and have to fall. Thus all are saved; for all have some ideas they are quite right upon. That is all there is to anybody, viz. his accurate ideas.

Jewish Ideas of Deity

The Jewish religion should have "a fair miter" put upon its head. The Jewish idea of Deity was the most nearly right of any nation's idea. Thus it wore the miter. The miter was upon the highest idea that people had of God. They did not know their highest idea of God. This figure which Zechariah saw representing their doctrine as it stood to date, with prophecies for later on, did not tell him what they thought they held which should be their strength directly. He only said that it would bring forth "a branch" by and by, and all the iniquity of the people should be utterly wiped out in a day.

The "branch" was the Jesus Christ to come. He should crown the high statements of Jewish theology with still higher ones. His statements should lay hold upon the absolute. The absolute is sinless. The sinless should occupy the earth in the visible sight of all mankind. It should be visible to all in one day. This part of the prophecy is just about being fulfilled. It would have been fulfilled then on a higher plan than simply rebuilding the temple but for the persistency with which they refused to deny the inconsistencies of their reasonings.

Willingness to give up certain inconsistencies of our reasonings about Deity is the secret of instantaneous demonstration. All who are slow in seeing their true thoughts demonstrated will find one point of error upon which they are awfully tenacious. Being tenacious upon the point of seeing people get punished for their sins is a time knot. Suppose De Lesseos (Builder of the Suez Canal) and his confreres had some time since found that their complications had all resulted from one mistake they all had made in common. Then they had put their finger of spiritual knowledge upon that error and spoken to it from the spiritual standpoint as taught by the science of religion. By some miracle of interposition they would be saved from disgrace and their victims would be reimbursed.

Fruits of Mistakes

"O, but," you say, "they defrauded and must of necessity see the results of their wickedness." That is your opinion. If it were a running sore in your own body, caused by some mistaken idea you put out years ago, you would want it healed. You would not want the open shame and unmistakable stench of a whole body sore with the fruitage of a mistake. There is only one principle given under Heaven for a change of raiment, whether if flesh body or social body, and that is the principle of the unreality of all things in our life except our goodness.

There is nobody under any law compelling him to take the fruits of the mistakes. Martin Luther had a dream in which Satan came showing him a dreadful list of his sins; at first Martin was unhappy because he felt that he ought to pay the penalty of so much badness by suffering in hell. Suddenly he said to Satan: "There is one thing you have forgotten. The blood of Jesus Christ cleanseth from all sin." Then Satan hung his head and glided out.

There is always the blood of Jesus Christ ready to cleanse from any sin. Blood means accurate ideas flowing vigorously through the mind.

So if you do not get on very well with some line you may be pretty certain you are tenacious of something you had better give up. Maybe you think it is one thing to heal the physical body of disease and another to heal the world of poverty.

Give up that time knot. Poverty is as much a disease as rheumatism or tonsillitis. Maybe you
believe in laying up money for old age. That is a
hard knot to get tied up in. It will twist you swiftly
into old age and put off your power in healing. It
will make you quite disheartened at your progress
in spiritual understanding.

Maybe you think you can not be highly spiritual in that particular situation where you are
now placed. That is not true. You can be as highly
spiritual and as much united to the power of God
while you are assisting a surgeon in a hospital as
if you were shut up in an office healing patients by
prayers.

These are the ideas which keep many from re-
alizing   spiritual   harmony   and   happy
circumstances just as the tenacious belief in a
regular Satan and a regular hades, with a decid-
edly human deity when dealing with women and
aliens of the Jews of Zechariah's time put off the
absolute fulfillment of this vision to this age.

The prophet saw that every man as the highest
should "call his neighbor under the vine and under
the fig tree." There are two meanings here for us.
With the time-worn applications of Scripture texts
we will do nothing. They have not demonstrated
well. Let us take the two meanings here, which
will demonstrate well at once.

First, as God is impartial Goodness, call every
man, woman and child abundantly provided for.
Tell them they dwell under the vine and fig tree of

the bountiful goodness of the impartial God. If anything about them strikes you as contrary to that description deny it. It is our delusion. "Judge not after the sight of the eyes."

Second, as the mind that is good is the only mind, be clear-sighted enough to observe that if forty people sit down to mentally tell a man he is unfortunate or sick, it would not alter his health or circumstances a particle unless he should take some external methods to carry out their silent messages. Evil thoughts have not a single grain of strength by themselves. They have to be aided and abetted by outward efforts.

But if one little woman sits down and meekly tells this text concerning health and prosperity to anybody in the face of the earth his bodily health and human conditions will be healed. She will not need to speak a loud word, take the slightest external notice, give a single dollar, administer a single druggists pill, but the unfortunate will revive.

If you think differently from this, if you believe that evil thoughts have carrying potency unaided by speech or outward labors, do not keep wondering why you can not keep yourself well or times have changed so much for the worse. In the days of truth there is prosperity, according to the tenth verse of this chapter.

Inter-Ocean Newspaper, January 22, 1893

LESSON V

Spirit of the Land

Zechariah 4:1-10

Information taken from Review

The fifth lesson [manuscript missing] showed that meekness and persistence are two golden pipes through which an unction from on high passes into the soul of man to make him strong to endure. Be meek to the true doctrine, no matter who presents it or how it antagonizes the old one, which has not brought you strength or health or security. Be persistent to hold that the spiritual nature of man is identified entirely with the Spirit that is God. Mighty signals will fly from the high tower where your heart abides. Miracle after miracle of kindness will be shown you. "And He whose hands have laid the foundations, His hands shall also finish it, and thou shalt know that the Lord of Hosts is with thee."

LESSON VI

Dedicating the Temple

Ezra 6:14-22

Information taken from Review

In the sixth lesson [manuscript missing] how plainly it is written: "The Jews prospered through the prophesying of Haggai." Never prophesy evil or failure for anybody or anything. It will seem to come to pass, but the chain around the neck of the man who bears your prophecy will drag hardest at your neck. He will be innocent and you will be guilty according to the law of the word. Innocence has a law unto itself of slipping the leash of hardships imposed by others. It is buoyed by a principle the guilty have not discovered. Notice the buoys near the harbors, how in the seething waters they swing and sink. Take the whole world and to it prophesy the highest, the happiest, the freest life your kindness can name. "Despise not prophesying."

LESSON VII

Nehemiah's Prayer

Nehemiah 13

Pericles and His Work in Building the Parthenon

At about the date of this lesson Pericles was building the Parthenon. There was only one street of Athens upon which he was ever seen. He found that if he would be utterly and supremely his best he must attend to his thoughts. When Newton was asked how he accomplished so much he said: "By intending my mind." An old school reader opened with the words, "Attention is the secret of success." By reason of neglect of the avenues from source to supply, the walls of Jerusalem had been broken down by enemies and the gates thereof had been burned with fire.

If we have nobody and nothing external to assist us, and after a season of heartfelt prayer we are helped into the achievements we pray for, we most certainly see the relation of prayer to our success.

Nehemiah insists that those Jews for whom the miracle of building the temple had been performed had, after about seventy-years, neglected the commandments and statutes and judgments, signifying their relation to their Provider and Champion. He sees that by such neglect they had really earned their broken fortunes. But he remembers one of the most beautiful principles of the relation of supreme goodness, if after our adversities begin which our forgetting brought about, we will then turn and remember we shall be instantly returned into favor. All our forgetfulness will be blotted out. We shall be reinstated with as quick results to our right principles as if we had been steadily faithful.

The long-time faithful have sometimes felt that it was unfair for those who came in at the eleventh hour to receive equal wages with them, but such is the nature of high principle that the mathematician who has neglected his figurings for many years will get just as correct solutions to his problems if he suddenly takes up his pencil and goes ardently to work and makes no mistakes in his reasonings, as the one who has plodded on for years without stopping.

The main thing seems to be giving the right proportion of attention due from us to principle. We may not be easily made one with the principle we are dealing with and thus can not accomplish as much in a given time with our reasonings as some others. Some mathematicians need to keep calculating all the time to keep their minds limber, while others spring to that which the others must practice for without any spur of use. There is no telling how much farther on in great discoveries those who neglect might have gone, by constant attention, than those faithful with they who are exactly equal, so when we neglect the means of keeping ourselves in continual harmony with the provider and healer of nations and then return to that relation again the simple answer to our realized need may be far indeed from the ecstasy of understanding which works miracles beyond such miracles that we would have had by perpetual fidelity.

Supreme Goodness

Nehemiah prays here reminding the supreme goodness of its never laying up any remembrance of our wrongdoing. All is as we ourselves choose. If we choose to leave on thinking high thoughts and prefer low ones, when we come to high thoughts again we shall find them just as efficient as ever if we are ready to receive them exactly as we did before. Principles are changeless. Principle is one and the same yesterday, today and forever.

The prophecy of Zechariah concerning two who should help in the building if the temple for Zerubbabel was fulfilled. The olive tree signifying perpetual renewal of two to help the temple forward means the spiritual principle from whose promulgation there should always be strength enough to work ardor in the minds of a certain type. Again we find Ezra and Artaxerxes. One was in power in prayer and the other the external operator. Wherever there is power in prayer somebody arises to carry out the external operations thereof.

Again, in these Nehemiah chapters, it is Nehemiah and Artaxerxes. All work we wish to see brought to pass is the building of a temple. It will certainly arise if we call upon the Most High Principle to unite with us. By us forever is the highest Helper in every task. Addressing ourselves unto it is to understand its ways. If we pray we shall slowly or swiftly take idealistic and unworldly methods for bringing out our achievements. For the invisible Helper whose name is God goes not by ordinary performances if we have submitted our works unto His judgment. "My ways are not your ways saith the Lord."

When Ezra started for Jerusalem he went without the usual military escort. He had preached confidence in God and would accept no other defense. Nehemiah felt that a military escort was the gift of Jehovah. So in healing the body; so in being provided for. Some who address themselves to the Divine principle feel that they must not take any external helps toward recovery. Others feel that all external helps are gifts of Jehovah. In casting themselves on the providing Jehovah some think they must not work for their living that is presented as the gift of Jehovah.

On and Upward

For ages mankind has urged itself onward and forward with terrible exertions. All great achievements they have argued have been wrought out through intense effort and unabated hardship. This is God's gift to man they say.

"Life evermore is fed by death,

In earth and sea and sky,

And that a rose may breathe its breath

Something must die."

This doctrine has been preached till it has covered the springing love of mercy in the race heart. None of it is true. All the good that has ever been wrought out of struggle came from the faith of the struggler. And faith is the still, small voice. All the life that has seemed to be fed by death has been by the faith in life felt by somebody. And faith is the eternal life that is Jehovah himself. Nobody was ever strengthened by the eating of meat, and nobody was ever healed by the application of material means. Nobody was ever defended by a sword or a gun. Nobody was ever provided for by noble endeavor. All is the product of faith. Whether it is truer to increase faith or increase struggle choose ye.

Nehemiah asks for prosperity for the cause he has undertaken. He is prosperous enough personally. He has great abilities and honorable position among men. But he would love to see all men prosper by knowledge of God direct. It is one thing to strike, as it were, hit or miss, upon prosperity, another to understand the principle whereby all may alike prosper in the Lord. Today that is exactly where the Christian must stand. He must teach Jesus Christ in such a way that by receiving his instruction all may live in strength, health, peace, prosperity, or he is running along in the old grooves and the world may go on hidden by its blind belief in him as in his predecessors.

In truth we may be sure there is no misery for one and happiness for another. In truth you may rely upon it where there is not sickness for one and health for another. If it seems so upon the earth then truth is not preached.

Inter-Ocean Newspaper, February 12, 1893

LESSON VIII

Ancient Religions

Nehemiah 4

Some of the Best Things Found in One of the Most

Ancient Religions

The Chinese

The ancient Chinese had a religion of the triad. The Tao-te-King thus speaks:

"You look for the Tao, and see it not. Its name is I.

You listen for it and do not hear it; its name is Hi.

You touch it, and do not feel it; its name is Wei.

These three are inscrutable and inexpressible.

We combine them in oneness, -which has no body — a form without form, an image without an image.

These inscrutable three are but one.

The Tao produced one; one produced two; the two produced three;

43

the three produced all beings."

Plato said: "God is three-fold: first as the profound, inscrutable substance and cause of all things; next as magnifying Himself in the ideas which are roots in the spiritual world; and thirdly, as the life of the universe. According to Pythagoras, "the first one was above all being; the second one contained the ideas of all being; the third one was the soul of all being."

According to the natural rendering of the native certainty of every mind; there is Good beyond our ideas of God; then our ideas of God; then the world according to our ideas by God's relation to it. In the idea of God, we have fatherhood; sonship, motherhood.

In this description we now speak of Father, Son, Holy Ghost. The Holy Ghost or Holy Spirit is the mother principle of the Godhead. All power in work is quickened by the Holy Ghost. All outward expression of power or achievement along any line is made by the sonship. The source of all is the Fatherhood. Yea there is but one God and His name is One.

The Sonship continually gives thanks and glad praises that God hath given the Holy Spirit the quickening life of universal Seeing that this is so, the Son breathes afresh of quickening life and demonstrates life that no death can touch. Jesus Christ recognized the life of the Holy Spirit, gave joyous thanks for it, and as recognizing it is demonstrating Sonship he was manifestly the Sonship of the Godhead.

The Chinese

The Chinese ancient poetists felt this principle and wrote it down as nearly as they could express themselves. It gave them added intelligence and skill. They learned by such a principle being held in mind how to make gold and how to prolong life hundreds of years, how to heal the sick instantaneously and how to be free from temptation.

The Sonship continually gives thanks and glad praise that God hath given the Holy Spirit the quickening health elixirs of the whole universe, and as recognizing this is being identified with it the Son breathes the divine elixir of spiritual health.

Jesus Christ thus became manifest Sonship of the Godhead and noticed the world that touched or saw him. Being alive forever and forever in conscious recognition of the Holy Spirit's nature as health, those who touch Jesus Christ with their character or with their thoughts get a charge from his health elixirs, and they also are Sonship of God, made manifest in health.

Any who recognize that all power is the power of the Holy Spirit and give thanks to gladness therefore, feel the thrills of power that Jesus Christ felt and are one with him in that measure they feel the power of the Holy Spirit. Jesus said that all Power had been received by him. That was because he was full of recognition of the nature and office of the motherhood of the Godhead as the quickening energy of the Universe.

Nehemiah in his prayer felt the touch of the comforter sent from God and became alive with the Jesus Christ understanding so that he undertook the rebuilding of the wall of Jerusalem.

The Holy Spirit

He had quickened his life and mind by feeling the breath of the Holy Spirit so that he could find a certain number of men and women with helping fervor by this speech. He was manifestly by the Sonship of God so far that undaunted by opposition, ridicule, slander, poverty, feebleness, and lewdness, he persevered.

Had he been entirely the Sonship of the Godhead made visible he would not have kept part of his building force "standing with spears in hand from the rising of the morn till the stars appeared." Lest enemies tear down their work and slay their families. For he who is manifestly the Son of God says, "Put up a sword into its sheath." He hath angels by myriad hosts at His side who disarm foes without his exertions or tremblings.

Whoever have saved a city from the violence of armies by warfare and bloodshed has recognized so little of the defending power to the Holy Spirit that he is far from demonstrating the Sonship of the Godhead, even though every city on the globe is a monument of this great prowess.

For the knowledge of the motherhood to the Godhead bring safety and bounty and joy without contest of any kind. The motherhood of the Godhead is love. Love casteth out fear. Love thinketh no evil.

Nehemiah told them (see Neh. 4) that they must not be afraid. That was recognition of the Comforter. So far he was Jesus Christ who feared nothing and felt safe walking over the planet, which put forth every uninspiring exertion to destroy him. Then Nehemiah said, "Remember the Lord which is great and terrible."

Here you have seen plainly that he dragged in his own idea of God along with Good. For God is not terrible. God is gentleness; God is the innocence of childhood; God is defenseless peace. But "God is great," was the absolute truth. Then he shouted to them to fight for their homes and families.

Poor human beings: I'm a man with one gleam of recognition of the presence and character of the motherhood of the Godhead speaks, they are so hungry for more of that mother that they take all that he says and does as part of that mother ministry. If he says "Slay" they spring to kill. If he says fight! They haste to obey.

There is one religion that teaches that by recognizing for his own self what God hath made as the quickening property of the Holy Spirit, each man will live and act, speak and achieve without swallowing the chaff, while the wheat of the other men's recognition of the Holy Ghost principle.

Inter-Ocean Newspaper, February 19, 1893

LESSON IX

UNDERSTANDING IS
STRENGTH

Nehemiah 13

Part 1

When the strongest eagle has flapped her great wings, their six labors of power, she folds them close and lies on the blue waves of the upper airs at rest. But her rest is her progress as much as her work. For rest is God as truly as activity is God. Therefore the fowls of the air heed the commandment *Festina Lente* (make haste slowly).

"The fox must sleep sometimes

The wild deer must rest."

Wherefore? For, swiftness in flight. Mind Is God. "And God rested on the seventh day." Thus mind thinks at its strongest best six movements thereof and on the seventh it forgets easily, gathers not willingly, and may accuse itself of age or overwork, when it is only resting at its seventh watch post.

If mankind would discern the signs of their own times they would drop the clutch of their hopes on the future when they feel the question, "What shall happen unto me?" stirring them, instead of rousing to newer zeal in effort to lay up for the future. They would let the mind lie still. Then for them there would surely be no time ahead with its feebleness, and languor so significant always of not having kept their Sabbath days wholly.

From earliest times the idea of the Sabbath rest for the body has obtained. It was the unconscious symbolization of that seventh period of mind which when it cometh with all its beauty of meaning men complain of as not clear, not strong, not at its best. And so we as a world are meant by this Nehemiah thirteenth lesson.

The governor of thought leaves the thoughts to act according to all the judgments given in wisdom, and speaks not at all during its onward march toward home, as Nehemiah left the Israelites for a season.

How should thoughts proceed when our quickening judgment .seems to have left us to the mechanical routine of our days? Exactly according to the highest ideals recognized by us when our noblest judgment spoke within us.

Do not let us be surprised if when we have prodded our mental energies to newer combats at times when we should have folded them for renewal. Nehemiah, the governor of our energies, returns and compels us to give up our thinking processes by painful interference. For Nehemiah appeared suddenly among those who had been selling all kinds of wares on the Sabbath day and shut the gates of Jerusalem, laying violent hands on all such as even waited outside the gates to buy or sell on the sly.

Thus we see that there is no compromise to be made with our mental energies when it is the time of their silence. The governor of our life will not say that the Sabbath is our period for thinking new thoughts or making new plans. It is the time of falling in with the sweep of our past thoughts as they are silently building around us their own kind of walls.

Taking this action of Nehemiah from the external standpoint it is very plain that historically he might be written of as exceedingly zealous in the matter of keeping the Sabbath day holy unto the Lord after the strictest ideas the Jews had held of the fourth commandment. But each Bible lesson has a deeper, more interesting and more uplifting significance than the opinions of men, and the history of governments. Each lesson means the life and mind of each one of us. It has to do with the greatest principles the divinest minds have expressed, and tells of the practical outcome of those principles when held firmly.

Here Nehemiah would seem to hold a very different idea of the province of the Sabbath from the teachings of Jesus Christ. Did not Jesus Christ say, "The Sabbath was made for man and not man for the Sabbath?" How, then, could Nehemiah be a man pleasing unto the God of Jesus Christ and make the men of Judah obey the Sabbath, as though they were made for it and not it for thorn? It was his blind obedience to an instinct or spiritual prompting which he knew as right, but, did not know how to teach. So far as he went in his mind he was consistent.

Today there are many high reasons why certain high usages are right, but there is nobody yet telling why they are generically right, nor where they lead out, nor what is their reality.

In the Royal Theatre at Copenhagen they have pantomimic portrayals of the rough life of the twelfth century in Denmark. After performing the most unchristian deeds and plotting with most unchristian venom, they kiss the cross of the Lord Jesus Christ. Should not years of usage of that symbol walk the feet of the Danish people nearer to the reality of what that cross signified? Are they not now nearer to the unwarlike tendencies of Him upon whom for ages they have vaguely thought? Shall they not by still thinking upon Him for whom the cross stands come still nearer by handling it as time goes on.

So with keeping the Sabbath. Rest on that day is a symbol in its ways of the rest of the mind from its six labors of bringing forth renewals of power. It is also symbolic of the rest from effort which the understanding of spiritual doctrine is to its people. He who enters into understanding of spiritual realities no longer struggles to accomplish the works of Jesus Christ. He is not staggered by the insistence of the doctrine of Jesus that if we do not preach the gospel, heal the sick, cast out passion, and raise the dead, we are not Christians. He can do these works and he does not have to try to do them. This is the rest of God in his mind which the Sabbath typifies.

By keeping still in his bodily practices one day out of seven he vaguely appreciates at first that there is some meaning for such a halting spot in his week. If he keeps it up he begins to think consciously why the Sabbath is ordained. When he finds that it is a symbol of the power of his own mind to do all things without effort he sees that it is from first to last a blessed gift.

When he realizes that all that the world is now doing is filled with the promise of rest to the world wherein all its powers and wisdoms and blessings shall come in their beauty and abide with every creature without striving and struggling to attain them, he is still more in love with the Sabbath.

Was Whittier conscious of all this when he sang the prophecy:-

"Evil shall cease and violence pass away,

And the tired world breathe free through a long Sabbath day."

Then when we appreciate why Nehemiah, Governor of Judah, punished those who would not keep the Sabbath, and realize that we put off the day of our highest life powers by not ceasing from trying to think when the mind is ready to fold her wings, we do not condemn Nehemiah for unconsciously symbolizing the natural shutting up of the gates against our memory and originality which we ourselves do. We see that the bird that would fly far must not move her wings every instant.

And if now we realize that the mind has her regular halting spots as the days have their Sabbaths, we shall be willing to learn which of the peculiarities of our own mind are symbolized by the one day in seven. There is one signal given to each of us when we are not to try to do or to be. Let us learn it.

And if now we find by the fine teaching of this lesson that Providence always brings out the prosperities in all ways more quickly and more satisfactorily by our using the Sabbath of our mind, shall we not love to keep it wholly?

Even in the blind and misinterpreted use of the symbol we shall always find ourselves more advantaged by the keeping of a Sabbath. A rough sea captain would not put into port to load his ship with a cargo on Sunday, but kept on his course with his ship to the disgust of his mate. They sailed on and a great storm arose which threatened to shipwreck the vessel. The storm was the means of their putting into a new port, loading up with a cargo of better quality; and getting home in three days less time than they would if they had stopped at the usual port on Sunday. The rough old captain could trace the metaphysical connection between his Sabbath rest, and his gained advantages.

And this brings us to the question as to what is expected of us on the Sabbath time, signified by the absence of Nehemiah from Jerusalem, for a whole people and by the periodic divisions of time which they had neglected during his absence.

Take the captain's example. He was obliged to sail on in the open sea, but he would not change his course. We do not enter upon new enterprises, nor increase or change our obligatory duties. If we do we detain ourselves on our march toward home. The detention is Nehemiah arriving and confusing our efforts.

All feebleness and languor of mind are signs of not having given the mind its Sabbath days. All forgetfulness and weariness of mind are signals of not having kept the Sabbath. Old age is a sign of not having kept the true Sabbath. Death is a signal that we have not heeded our mental Sabbaths. Forgetfulness, insomnia, old age, death, are the violent hands of the law laid upon us. The law is always our friend. But it is not an agreeable friend. When we cross it, we do not get free from the law by defying the law, but by keeping the law.

We do not get the refreshment and strength of our mind by exercising it when its nature says rest, but by resting.

In the progress of mind with spiritual doctrines we are often discouraged at the slowness with which we get on. At that moment we must not think of ourselves or of the doctrine. Let them alone. Give up trying to understand it. Give up caring whether you understand or not. If it is true, and you have thought it out, so far you have done your part. With the results you have nothing to do. This is your mental Sabbath.

If now you cry or fret or droop it is evidence you did not begin your mental Sunday early enough. You will see by the nineteenth verse that "when the gates of Jerusalem began to be dark before the Sabbath" Nehemiah began to interfere with the non-Sabbatical Jews. This certainly means that if we observe the actions of our own minds we shall see that it has vehement zeal for six movements and then is not interested for a season. Keeping those movements we get into the port of life without weariness or death. It is now long past the time when we ought to have ceased from our toils. Not only did the dark strike the gates of our city a long while ago, but the day is far past. All these things that are now happening unto us would never have happened if we had kept our Sabbath in mind.

All things are in thought before they are in externals. We had to feel that we must keep at our planning for the future and keep at it, and believe in a future still needing our attention before the failure and drooping of our bodies could set in. Man feels that he must prepare for the time to come by unremitting exertions. The very thinking that this is the law of success is the "dark on the gates". He is loading himself in mind with a night that would never come if he would here, at the point where he even begins to think of what he must do for his future, think nothing at all. Here is where the eagle folds his wings and lets the journey onward take care of itself.

"He who from zone to zone

Guides through the boundless air

The wild bird's trackless flight,

In the long wait that I must tread alone,

Will surely guide my steps aright."

Inter-Ocean Newspaper, February 26, 1893

LESSON X

UNDERSTANDING IS STRENGTH

Nehemiah 13

Part 2

It is the rest of the mind to know that God cares for us all as the sparrows are cared for. It quickens the mind at its right intervals to originality and noble achievement to have for a confidence the principle, "He careth for me." To believe with simple trust that our life is divinely ordered, is to work on six days as the genius works, and to cease from all efforts, yet be accomplishing all things.

To know this principle is a rest to the mind, which will soon show out in refreshment of body. To love it is to have our "strength renewed like the eagle," To understand it is to usher us into the country where "there is no night there" no death, no drooping, no crying, no faltering. The doctrine of rest is the Sabbath idea of the mind. Let us speak of the doctrine of rest.

The world now feels the hurts of the law inter-
fering with its ignoring the Jesus Christ teaching
of what a loving gift is the Sabbath to man, as the
Jews felt the reforms of Nehemiah. The Sabbath to
man is the doctrine of casting our care. This part
of the Jesus Christ teaching having been ignored,
we have been one great Sabbath-breaking world.
We have bound heavy burdens and laid them on
our shoulders when we ought to have been free.

We have believed in preparing for old age, and
this was loading ourselves on the Sabbath. We
have believed that we must crowd our minds with
thoughts of things and their operations instead of
with principles, and this was breaking the Sabbath. We have believed that all men must die, and
so must we, and have taught each other to prepare
for death, and this was breaking the Sabbath. We
have thought that if we did not keep incessant
guard we should lose our friends, our places, our
honors, our loved ones, and this was breaking the
Sabbath.

Job tells us that "the hypocrite's hope shall
perish". So if a human being smiles and smiles
while his heart is heavy within him he will have
many disappointments. But the beauty of such
hypocrisy is that by and by the smiles train the
heart to their practices and the heart smiles with
the face. Then there is no longer any hypocrisy in
the smiling and the hopes cone into happy fulfillment.

While we are in the bitter seas of perishing hopes we lift up our hearts and voices in unison, asking with undivided mind for help and sustaining. We are so whole-souled at such times that we forbid the least hint of doubt to creep into our mental premises. So the help or sustaining is forthcoming. Then we relapse into our divided mind again, and again sail the dark waters of failure of hopes.

Somebody has written that the only hell there is is the failure of a great purpose. But to him whose heart's love and every thought and word are set to great purpose there is no failure. Enjobo, the Buddhist priest, set his mind to learn how to defeat the God of poverty. He thought about it for years and practiced everything he had ever read or heard of to see wherein lay the secret of overcoming poverty as disease can be overcome, by spiritual force instead of by slow, hard economy or fortunate transactions.

On the last night of the last month of a year a formula came into his mind, and reciting it in concert with other priests he succeeded. From that hour he was prospered in all his ways,

In all things this law obtains, Nehemiah succeeded in rebuilding the Jerusalem wall because he was no hypocrite. All that he had he gave to the cause. He kept back none of his money, none of his time, none of his talents, none of his thoughts. And therefore "in all that he did he prospered, because his heart was in it."

61

And now all the people are gathered together as one man to hear the old law read. Nehemiah's enemies are astounded that he has succeeded through such obstacles as they have thrown in his way. Zerubbabel, Ezra, Nehemiah, stand out on the pages of history as living examples of the irresistible power of sincere purpose withholding nothing. They saw in their day the prosperity of their cause.

To what cause are you pledged, and how much do you withhold from carrying it out? What you withhold is the secret of your stoppages, defeats, disappointments. While the days speed on without miseries are you as devoted to your religion as in those surging trial times when what you had heard of spiritual laws you put so intensely into practice?

Take notice of the first axiom of life according to Jesus, "Thou shalt love the Lord thy God with all thy heart and with all thy soul, and with all thy mind and with all thy strength; this is the first commandment."

There is nothing here about dividing your attention between high purpose and no purpose, not anything about resting upon the intentness of mind to the one theme to which you are pledged as a student of spiritual principles.

Standing by the side of the devoted Ezra were a number of readers of the law whose names appear this once in history as helpers of the Scribe and then they, fall into oblivion-. Doubtless they were far more eager than Ezra or Nehemiah to be recognized as great among their contemporaries and in after times, but they could not forego the habits and inclinations of their times and associates. They have fallen like the leaves of a tree, not failures, not evil, not weak, not despised, but nothing in demonstration of their possibilities. So does each age find only a few giving heart and soul and mind and strength and time and money to the cause they have espoused, These few stand to the many as trees to the leaves in a forest. Generations come and generations go, but they live on forever.

Then Nehemiah taught the people that on their holy days they should rejoice and give thanks, and "mourn not nor weep." Read over the eighth chapter of Nehemiah and see if you do not catch the uplifting breezes of Nehemiah's undaunted spirit to this day. He who had cause to mourn when he so plainly saw the readiness with which the people veered from high idea to low idea as the sound of a positive voice lifts up his strong soul to touch the keystone of God's will to man, and bids them all rejoice with them in the Lord their strength. There is a vitalizing and inspiring sound to the words, "The joy of the Lord is your strength," especially when uttered from the heart of a lover of goodness and a steadfast adherent to a principle. Notice with what confident tones the voice of a successful human being speaks. He inspires confidence.

So the people ceased from weeping because they had been so negligent of the law and rejoiced that the everlasting God was their daily strength and sure reward. They gave freely of their provisions to such as had never believed in success along any lines. By such giving they communicated the joy of Nehemiah to even the beggars.

Here is a great principle as related to giving and receiving. As we touch the money that comes from the prosperous man's hands we feel more or less his mental attitude toward money. If we read the faint hieroglyphics of his unconscious thoughts on the coin, we catch the whole secret of his ways of thinking which bring him such plenty. So the beggars might learn the whole law of prosperity.

This is on the mental plane as related to material things. It is exactly as people caught the conscious thoughts of Paul when his clothing was handled by them and were healed. It is like as Jesus caused the threads of His garments to set the blood currents into happy health if one only touched their hem. So here Nehemiah's joy of heart, with its omnipotent strength, if persisted in, kindled joy in the Levites, who lighted the hearts of the house-holders, and they gave of their substance to the joyless and kindled their slow fires into new flame till there was one great thanksgiving day in Jerusalem.

It is not the provisions we give to those who seem to be poor that help them to satisfaction; it is the touch of our way of giving they catch. It is not a help to them if we do not communicate with our provisions a joy of heart. Much contribution to church and charity and school does not accomplish the purpose if the heart goes not with the giving. A penny with the communicable letters of a joyous spirit stamped upon it will carry the mystery; of strength in its crevice and many a one will wonder why he feels equal to meeting the tasks of his day when he has had no good news and nothing has been fed to him calculated to make him forget his sore lot.

So smile and rejoice and give thanks and praise God whether your heart is with it or not, for by and by your good will conquer the claims of the flesh and of fate and the strength of unity of mind and heart and speech shall be yours. Understanding is strength. He that hath ears to hear this doctrine can understand it .and you will see by this chapter that the people who listened to Nehemiah understood and obeyed.

Inter-Ocean Newspaper, March 5, 1893

LESSON XI

WAY OF THE SPIRIT

Esther

In one of Ibsen's plays, "An Enemy of Society", he makes a character affirm that "the strongest man in the world is he who stands most alone." A step beyond his "strongest man in the world" is he who with least assistance and most depending upon Him, accomplishes his undertakings. There have been men who held the destinies of a multitude in the hollow of their hand and with the world against them, in the name of a God whose assistance to His people is only a tradition with them, met the world and won their cause.

Thus Esther, a star in historic skies brilliant with great woman's names, shines brightest. Thus David the shepherd boy, with his ever-increasing power to inspire us with simple trust in that God who works best for those with simplest faith. Thus Jesus, on the borderline between time and eternity, met captivity itself and practically, for the sake of a world, proved the belief in death and sin

to be man's belief in what cannot exist in the omnipresent Being of God.

Between the years 469 and 467, B.C., Xerxes,
the Persian King, gave Haman, his high counsel-
lor, permission to destroy all the Jews scattered
about the Persian empire. Haman bought the
honor for about $20,000,000. It has been in all
times an extraordinary imitation of greatness on
the part of mortal ambition to advance itself high
on the banners of fame by degrading or stepping
upon the necks of the greatest numbers possible.
We have the same exhibitions nowadays, when our
Hamans get large sums of money and buy off society, our modern Persian king, the recognized right
to "grind down the faces of the poor" by modern
methods.

And as yet no Esther or David has appeared to
meet King Public Acquiescence in battle array
"with weapons not carnal but mighty through God
to the (instantaneous) pulling down of strong-
holds."

All who have fought modern society, which
sells out such stupendous privileges to its Hamans, have donned the armor of the world's
methods and got defeated, exactly as David would
have been defeated if he had met Goliath in the
King's armor; exactly as Esther would have been
defeated had she been a fed and petted beauty
instead of a holy maiden dedicated to a mighty
purpose.

How powerless, imbecile, absent, seemed Goliath under the sling-stone of David. How weak, *compos mentis (of sound mind), non est (not to be found)*, seemed Haman under the light of Esther's white countenance. How incompetent, negative, nowhere, shall be the powers of this age raised against the seemingly defenseless when the prophecy of Daniel stands in its stately splendor here in our midst. "And at this time shall Michael stand up, the great prince which standeth for the children of thy people, and at that time thy people shall be delivered and the God of Heaven shall set up a kingdom which shall never be destroyed, and the kingdom shall not be left to other people, but it shall break in pieces and consume all these kingdoms, and it shall stand forever."

The Ahasuerus of Esther was the Xerxes who set forth with an army of more than 5,000,000 men to punish the Athenians for their defeat of his father, Darius, at Marathon, and returned with scarcely 5,000 soldiers, after being defeated at Thermopylae by Leonidas and his 300 and at Salamis in a naval engagement, when Themistocles with 300 vessels overcame his 2,000 and in other battles wherein he had shown his incompetency to hold his own when pitted against the ethics of life.

Xerxes can conquer Egypt but not Greece. The fire of genius cannot be bought or coerced, but sordid materiality can be both bought and forced. Xerxes was like a reed in the wind of the prayers of the Jews. Religion at its truest does without effort, instantaneously, what intellect at its highest power has to fight desperately to attain even a sign of.

Genius has generally fought hard for even its bread and bed. It has seldom had kindly shelter at Society's jeweled hand. Names that posterity will honor are unheard of in our midst. This is the way of the seeming world; what has been called the "shadow system,"

In this story of Esther we have been told how, in the dream of materiality, one ray of true spiritual doctrine, one gleam of real confidence in Spirit, will accomplish any object ordained by the mind. Mordecai gave to Esther the whole secret of fulfillment of prayer when, in begging her as Queen to stand in that place where was none ever permitted to stand and live, he said: "Enlargement and deliverance shall arise to the Jews." He spoke the faith of a people. By faith the very dead are raised. By faith, even a very little faith, a mountain will remove and be cast into the sea.

But Esther had not Mordecai's faith. God was to her a tradition. She had never known any miracle to be wrought for the Jews by their God. She had been kept in the harem of a fierce and merciless king. How should she know but that the God who was capable of letting her people get so close to cruel death might be capable of letting them pass through its teeth?

That one is greatest who with most depending upon him has least assistance in his undertaking.

Esther had not even faith. Therefore Mordecai said: "Who knoweth whether thou art come to the kingdom for such a time as this?" She had not even Mordecai's confidence. Lonely child of destiny! Therefore she fasted and prayed. Instead of faith came a great calm. It was the calm of an unattended soul walking in truth.

"All truth is calm, refuge and rock and tower,

The more of truth the more of calm;

Its calmness is its power."

Was she not true to her highest? That is the only truth for any of us. What was that light that shone from Esther's face that made the King signal that instead of death she should have life? When one is true to his place, true to his calling, true to his highest conception of what is right, there is deathless divinity shining through him. There is no Persian King who can touch him. "He shall be safe from the arrow that flieth."

How mysterious is the way of the Spirit given its free highway over the doings of men by the faith of the good! Faith is the substance over which the armies of spirit walk to conquer the purpose of evil not by bloodshed, not by pain and terror, but swiftly, all in a night, by ways as natural as the rising of the sun, "Evil shall be destroyed, and that without hand."

Even when this omnipotent soul had the opportunity to speak she did not ask that which she might have asked. Hers was the inspiration of

71

silence. Then the King was disturbed in his sleep. How natural it seems. So natural does it seem when after having felt as if dissolution were setting in, you have arisen with the morning refreshed and renewed The white tenderness of some healing thoughts has rested on your head as you slept; the love or the gratitude of some innocent child has followed you and pleaded your cause with the spirit of healing and you did not know it,

"I drew them with the bands of love and they knew not that I healed them." "Every good and perfect gift is from above." The King's eye lights on the record of a scroll where Mordecai is mentioned as having interposed to save his life. Suddenly he asks what favor has been granted this noble Mordecai. "None," they tell him. And the next day Mordecai is led in triumph through the city of the King's winter-palace, as defender of royalty, set above Haman who has bought permission to slay him. And so the Jews live. All this is forerunner. It is antitype of our own times.

Faith is not wakened, not quickened, in the hearts of those who have only heard what great things the Lord hath done. They have not seen it; yet they are true to the highest they have seen, to the noblest they can see. Strong people believe in the deliverance of mankind from the hard lines of today's combinations. They believe that in true religion is to be found the way out of the bondage of sin, sickness, death, ignorance, fear. They do not think they themselves are the ones to bring the deliverance to pass. They believe it is those who are peculiarly called to stand in pulpits, on platforms — those dangerous "inner courts" of society where "who shall stand and live?" Yet the people are not sure that after all it is the preaching of this hour. They have faith in the God of deliverance. They believe deliverance is coming, but the Esthers must go into the Courts alone.

Inter-Ocean Newspaper, March 12, 1893

LESSON XII

SPEAKING OF RIGHT THINGS

Proverbs 23:15-23

Delitzech, the Scripture commentator often quoted by the committee on International Bible lessons, says: "Wisdom is inborn in no one. Folly is bound up in the heart of a child, and it must be driven out by severe discipline." Evidently the writer of the verses composing the lesson for today was of the opinion that his child had inherited folly of heart, for he speaks of listening to the experiences of his father and mother, who before him had been very foolish, but had as they traveled on in life picked up a little wisdom.

When anyone carefully notes the teachings of Jesus Christ he knows better than to say "if thine heart be wise" to a little child, to a youth, or even to a grown-up man or woman. He remembers that Jesus said of children: "Their angels (thoughts) do always behold the face of the Father." He remembers that Jesus said: "Call no man upon the earth your father (origin of your nature), for One is your Father." Being mindful of Jesus he accuses not anybody, even in his heart, of being by nature different from God who generated him.

Solomon here in the sixteenth verse admits a principle which is but just coming to be recognized, viz., the effect of speech upon the physical body. The fifteenth verse gives the treatment which men and women have brought up their children on — "if thine heart be wise." That questioning attitude toward a child, the implied doubt as to its trend of mind, has been the "bending of more young people toward the shady side of conduct than all the "pleasing allurements of vice" (as poetry puts it).

Hear this writer admitting that his kidneys are healed, when in spite of his father's doubt of his native intelligence the son "speaks right things!" Is it not thus written, so plainly that he who runs may read, that if the positive speech of a child can cure the physical drooping of some organ of the body, the positive confidence of a parent in the God-inherited wisdom of his child may store the brain cells of his offspring with gray matter suffi- cient to teach a doctrine that will cure a world of ignorance and disease?

Parents long with inexpressible yearnings for their children to be good to occupy honored places in life, to be wise and prosperous. They are as afraid that they will not be all this that they train and push and drive their offspring continually. It is not those who hope that their children will do well, but fear they will not, who live and see them fulfilling their hopes; it is those who had confidence in them or left them free from their fears who hear of "the Lord's doing, so marvelous in our eyes."

Solomon intimates that some children slip the leash of the doubts of their parents, and, remembering the "glory of goodness and wisdom that they had with the Father before the world was," they say noble things with their lips. He agrees from his own experience that a malady peculiar to advancing years is absolutely cured, the debilitating microbes thereof are neutralized and the vigorous elasticity of youth is restored unto him by the words of a child s«t free from his father's doubts.

Then he shows that, though his son has shown signs that he knows the law of truth, it may be possible that in his secret heart he is slyly looking towards drinking, smoking, swearing, snobbery, etc., as much more enchanting practices than increasing the exhibition of his native genius. He begs, of his boy (whose thoughts according to Jesus, have been set on high always) not to envy the pleasures of sin. From his own experience with yielding he has no tint of hope in his mind that his son will stand to his God-born chastity.

This man who wrote these words may not be the Solomon of history, or he may: he certainly writes more as we would expect a Solomon to write

than any other kind of a man, for Solomon believed in holding on to this intelligence long after
he gave up believing in his power to hold on to his
holiness. Therefore he admits that his son may
possibly speak intelligently, but he has no hope
that he will be moral.

Socrates, upon being asked what was the most
trouble-some to good men, answered, "The prosperity of the wicked." How did Socrates know that
some men are more wicked than others? When
Paul was writing to Timothy once, he told him
that some men's sins are openly exposed, where all
the world can see them plainly, while other men's
sins follow after them not at all visible to their
neighbors. Inasmuch as fear that a child will do
something bad is pretty sure to make it do the
very thing, while the sight of a bleared face is sure
to disgust him, whose sin against the boy is worse
if it comes to a matter of choice?

In the twenty-first verse the teacher has re-
course to a lie in order to carry his point. If it was
indeed Solomon he might have expected that.
Rehoboam would turn his kingdom over to his
enemies if he told him that drinking, eating, and
such other accompanying performances as he himself, the great Solomon, was then practicing would
"clothe a man with rags and bring him to poverty,"
when the boy saw with his own eyes that it was no
such thing, as his father himself was evidence.
Was he not royally appareled? Was he not im-
mensely rich? Did not the earth do him reverence?

If anything would "bind Rehoboam, whose natural mind was set toward enlarging his kingdom in wisdom and holiness, to turn out as history records, it was such a lie as this.

In after time, when his son enlarges his enemies' possessions instead of his own, it was by reason of the mental attitude of his father towards him. To halt in mind between hope of your son's turning out right and fear that the world will be too much for him is a "treatment" you will see work out in irresolution of character. To boldly address the upright spirit of your son, fearlessly proclaiming its strength, its intelligence, its nobility, its goodness, ignoring the flesh nature which from its intellect to its feet you have been taught is "prone to err as the sparks fly upward," is to see that nature stand out in its uncompromising splendour. You had better leave him free from your trainings, as Mary left Jesus, than to train him because you fear for him, or to talk to him against his spiritual convictions.

"Hearken unto thy father that begat thee, and despise not thy mother when she is old." Thus reads the twenty-second verse. Our Father is God. Everything speaks of God. We have ears which, if we use them, will detect the voice of God. It is to those ears you speak when you describe the goodness and intelligence of one you are "treating". To speak mentally to the immortal nature of your neighbor is to see it come forth demonstrating your description. If you are treating a man whose beliefs of human laws have given him softened brain, do you as a Christian thinker describe him in your mind as an idiot, or as one needing to have some of the free intelligence there present given to him? No, you tell him his intelligence was never lost; it cannot be found; it is his internal fullness.

Thus you talk to your child and convey to his spiritual ears the truth which acts like leaven with his own nature. Truth is the Father. He who speaks truth is truth. Thus he who speaks truth is the Father. The Brahmins give a recipe for practicing spiritual thinking till we become spirit; for practicing the presence of God till we become God. One of the practices is listening. You do not need to have a great and noble mind think toward you to bring out your intelligence in its beauty. Sit still and listen — listen as you would listen for the footsteps of your beloved walking in Heaven-shod silence from the Kingdom of Peace.

Then shalt the trees that lean and whisper against the far horizons tell thee of thine own wonderful fitness to do some mighty work easily. Then shall the winds that blow from spiced Araby, and shrill from the white northlands, sing of thy right place and right mission on earth. Listen: God the Father speaks to thee. The repetition of true words is one practice: "hearkening" to thy Father's voice is another. Do not neglect either. You will not neglect either. This lesson is a voice speaking you will not ignore.

God the Father and God the Mother is one God. When sweet mercifulness touched thy life on days when thou hadst expected torture it was the motherhood of God speaking. When beauty and smiling prosperity came instead of the messages of calamity feared by thy heart, then was the motherhood of God speaking. When glad meetings have taken place after long estrangements, after hope was departed, then has the motherhood of God been speaking. The Holy Spirit of God, is the love, the mercy, the beauty, the tenderness of. God. When these touch thy life on days when thy heart is fainting with long-deterred good, then is the motherhood of God bending over thee. This Mother never grows old. Her kiss of tenderness faileth not through the generations. He who speaks of his mother shall call her the motherhood of God. His message to her shall be true as hers shall be true, and so fulfilling the law of truth, no Solomon will ever have to fear that a son shall "despise" a mother because "she is old."

Deafness of the physical ears is sign of protracted refusal to listen to the voice of the Spirit. You never saw a deaf man or woman whose tasks were not self-imposed. The real opportunities for leisure given them are the continual patience of the motherhood of the God-head trying with them to have them of free will stop from their intense will toward activity and sit still to listen — listen for the messages of the Spirit. There is sure cure for deafness in the persistent practice of listening with strained ears while entirely alone for every sound, smiling at the signal of the least new sound.   So there is cure for our heart's restlessness in our listening for the finer voices of the sounds of the universe.

The Easterners say the Westerners cannot listen, therefore such a large proportion of deafness. The Occident tells the Orient that they will not see obvious principles, therefore such a large proportion of blindness. They who listen can hear, "This is the way, walk ye in it." They who see the meanings, of spiritual doctrines see the beauty and brightness of love and kindness in all things. To them nothing is ever ugly from age, from disproportionateriess, from imperfection. To the deep eyesight of eternal God set free through them, "'All is Good."

The last verse of our lesson says, "Buy the truth." No matter what people say or do with you, truth is worth the price of their disfavor.

> *"For more than thou canst give to Truth Will she on thee confer."*

No matter how your doctrines are received put them forth with your soul in them. The new light, the new peace, the new mercifulness of life is worth the price. "Sell it not." Nothing tempts the mother to give away her child. Nothing tempts God to forsake His own, "When thy father and thy mother forsake thee, the Lord will pick, thee up." So nothing tempts the Spirit of man, set free over the pathways in which he must walk, to say that material conditions can burden the Spirit. The Spirit of man never says, "I am cast down," nor "I am bound with chains." The Spirit is free and untempted; fearless and untrammeled; Spirit is Omniscient God.

Inter-Ocean Newspaper, March 19, 1893

LESSON XIII

REVIEW

Historically considered, the lessons of the last quarter have revealed Bible events of important epochs. They touched the age of Herodotus, Socrates, Plato, and Yenophon. They included the dates of Marathon, Thermopylae, Salamis. Where Esther, the daughter of true religion unattended except by the angels, won her cause without bloodshed. Greece with her philosophy and imaginations of Deity spilled the reddest blood of her brave youth. And thus philosophy and religion looked into each other's faces and asked, "What of the night?"

The lessons are all sweetly subtle in their showings of how by the light of a knowledge of truth with respect to conquering principles, great deeds may be done without pain or discord. They are all the exemplification of the simple words of Jesus: *"Ye shall know the truth and the truth* shall *make you free."* They all teach that "the king is not saved by the multitude of an host". They all teach that *"it is not by power and not by might, but by My Spirit"* that man must work through the problems of poverty, disease, sorrow, bondage.

They all intimate that it is better to get acquainted with the Holy Ghost, who can "teach us all things and call all things to our remembrance", than to study the plastic arts, music, Egyptian hieroglyphics, etc., because by the study of these we lose our brains, our memory, our strength, instead of improving them.

They teach us that it would certainly pay somebody to undertake to live and know by communication with the Spirit of God instead of copying after so many billions of examples of undertaking to live and know by communication with material processes. For anything undertaken by anybody who fixed his mind on the Spirit throughout this period was successful in his enterprise, while no matter what apparent advantages their opponents had to set out with, they were always defeated. Moreover, the victors by reason of the Holy Ghost always conquered the heart and will with the seizure of gold and arms. Was not Xerxes led captive in heart and will by Esther, when Greece could only conquer his spears and soldiers?

How quickly the mighty victories of the spiritually-minded hastened over the roadways of time! So quickly when it is all past shall speed the time we have passed as human if we have worked out our own plan of campaign as spiritual, not material. What was true of Zerubbabel, Ezra, Nehemiah, Esther, shall be true of the whole race somewhere, somehow, sometime, for no one is without the same Spirit that moved them, though multitudes hide their spirit through the ages.

"Oh, now I know how all Thy lights combine

And the configurations of their stories,

Seeing not only how each one doth shine,

But all the constellations in their glory."

There are twelve propositions in the geometry of life here put before us for consideration. They all tend to one end as do all the propositions of Euclid. His goal to prove mathematics to be an exact science. These go to prove spiritual man omnipotent.

First Babylon seems to lead Israel captive, but as the Spirit is never led captive to that which is not Spirit, the true Israel was never led captive to Babylon. So, no matter how much intellectual attainments and social splendors hide the true heart of mankind, it is not ever amalgamated in truth. It thinks and cries out toward the divine. It never trusts Babylon. And this thinking toward the divine, which the heart keeps up forever, finally breaks forth into living faith. There are shining threads joining the heart of man to the heart that is God, that pull and pull till nations are overturned in a day; kingdoms rise and fall to make way for some swelling thought of the people who seem to be honoring the apparent sovereigns.

In the Parthenon at Paris there is a picture of Caesar entering Rome in triumph. Underneath are the catacombs, and in the dim light Christiana are praying. So the empire was undermined by martyrs' prayers. Everything works to carry out the heart's highest aspiration. There is cause for rejoicing that such a law reigns. In a classroom in a certain school, when one of the students asked the sincere-looking professor if he thought that there could be an aspiration without a means of carrying it out, as there could not be fins without water to fulfill their aspirations, he answered that he believed such to be the divine provision of the beneficent Creator. Applause such as he had never received before burst on him. What his learned disquisitions, his memories of facts and theories had never brought forth, one touch on the glowing heart fires of youth elicited in full measure.

But age does not intermeddle with hope. Expectation of good never fails. The Buddhists believe that we try human existence again and again till we substantiate our highest hopes here on earth. Some of them believe that with the incoming of the tenth avatar one-fifth of the human race will suddenly demonstrate their expectations of absolute good.

"All crimes shall cease and ancient wrongs shall fail,

Justice returning lift aloft her scale,

And white-robed innocence o'er the earth prevail."

Then the globe is to shine clear as crystal. The thoughts of all hearts are to be revealed. In the Dhammapada, the history of the emergencies of spiritual liberty, Babylonian bondage is rendered thus: "Without ceasing shall I run through a course of many births, looking for the maker of this tabernacle, and painful is birth again and again. But now. Maker of the tabernacle. Thou hast been seen; Thou shalt not make up this tabernacle again. All Thy rafters are broken. Thy ridgepole is sundered; the mind, being sundered, has attained."

When Cyrus came, at a most unpropitious moment, judging from appearances, the longingly-looked-for freedom burst upon them. "Then the captive exiles hastened to be loosed." Let every heart that longeth for freedom know this, that those who did not understand the law of Spirit, that it makes toward freedom, mourned as those that could not be comforted, yet their freedom came. And those who do know this law of the Spirit need not mourn, for, knowing the law of Spirit, freedom makes haste.

The second point of the twelve propositions or lessons reiterates the idea that whatever premise or idea a man takes into his mind and makes dominant will act like a magnet to draw everything to sustain and externalize it. The Governor of Judea was the living representative of the idea of Cyrus that the temple at Jerusalem must be rebuilt. Through evil and good report, through misfortune and prosperity, the idea of the temple lived in mind till its foundations were finally laid.

This is a lesson like the keystone in the arch of a bridge. He who knows this proposition is already on the highway to success. Let a man take the idea or premise that there is a sure cure for consumption somewhere and by some means, and if he keeps looking around all the time for that cure he will charge his mind with curative potency which will increase and increase till some day it will bloom into the "discovery" of an infallible cure. The "discovery" will not be a discovery at all; it will be simply that just as his mind reached its bloom he was concocting some preparation which never had any such remedial energy before, but his quickened spirit now charges it with his degree.

A man has a secret thought against his own powers and against his intelligence. He thinks badly of himself. In the fullness of time he has gathered every force of his daily surroundings which could possibly contribute to externalize that premise he has taken. One day a car breaks down or a bank fails and he instantly goes crazy. Then people say that the bank failure or the fall injured him.

There is one man who has had a proposition intensifying for many years. It is charging itself with the right potency to bloom upon the world eventually as a water lily opens after a year's closed secrets. Lippincott's for last December says this of his proposition: "Twenty-six groups are completed, and when the twenty-seventh group is under equal control he expects to have established a circuit of vibratory force for running machinery both for aerial navigation and for terrestrial use. This man's purpose would have been in successful demonstration now if he had not been so free in telling about it to a mass of skeptical minds, thus spilling his reserves continually. This was the case with the second building of the temple at Jerusalem, as we find by the great delay thereof. What is your dominant wish? Do not let it any longer lie in your mind as a wish. Say, "It is so!" Say, "It must be so!" Say, "It shall be so!" Then keep your purpose to yourself. Turn every item over as it presents itself to see if it has any bearing on the externalization of your purpose. It will not wait for you to die to be carried out either, like the pious idea of preaching the gospel to the poor, viz., that they must wait for the after-life to be fed and housed and clothed properly, when Jesus Christ meant that those who understood His doctrine should never know poverty or want any more from the moment they understood His teachings.

A certain man has taken the idea strongly that it is better to study the God mind than to study books. He believes that by communion with the origin of all expressions of intelligence he shall thereby better express intelligence. One believes that by direct address to the health of the universe the way to instantaneous healing will be made plain to him. The history of all those who have, like Job, "maintained their cause", goes to show that nobody has to die before he is a success in his own line.

The third proposition of this science reads that even the tiniest event, your dreams, your passing acquaintances, your hindrances and expeditions plainly show how nearly your principal idea is to its fulfillment. They even tell what your principal secret idea is. It is not always the one you think it is, for you have the premise you wish to see soonest exhibited in the realm of wish.

The fourth lesson explained that one of the absolutely requisite steps toward the "seven-eyed visions" which the final prosperity of a noble premise gives, is the definite rejection of everything which disputes it. In logic we have "universal negative". If you need obstacles and oppositions of your lofty proposition, it will not fulfill on this plane of existence. You must do as the old-fashioned doctrine proclaimed, viz., wait till the next sphere.

This is the law under every circumstance and for every premise. The stone of rejection of all that opposes your loftiest proclamation is symbolized by the sapphire, the stone of peace. The text you remember at this point was: "I will remove the iniquity of that land in one day." Then all the earth shall sit in safety, "every man under the vine and fig tree" of prosperity, because by the science of God he knows his inheritance and how to lay hold of it.

The fifth lesson showed that meekness and persistence are two golden pipes through which an unction from on high passes into the soul of man to make him strong to endure. Be meek to the true doctrine, no matter who presents it or how it antagonizes the old one, which has not brought you strength or health or security. Be persistent to hold that the spiritual nature of man is identified entirely with the Spirit that is God. Mighty signals will fly from the high tower where your heart abides. Miracle after miracle of kindness will be shown you. "And He whose hands have laid the foundations, His hands shall also finish it, and thou shalt know that the Lord of Hosts is with thee."

In the sixth lesson how plainly it is written: "The Jews prospered through the prophesying of Haggai." Never prophesy evil or failure for anybody or anything. It will seem to come to pass, but the chain around the neck of the man who bears your prophecy will drag hardest at your neck. He will be innocent and you will be guilty according to the law of the word. Innocence has a law unto itself of slipping the leash of hardships imposed by others. It is buoyed by a principle the guilty have not discovered. Notice the buoys near the harbors, how in the seething waters they swing and sink. Take the whole world and to it prophesy the highest, the happiest, the freest life your kindness can name. "Despise not prophesying."

The seventh lesson teaches that civilization at its highest while the wrong idea of God is held in mind will be a failure; that it is almost instantaneous transformation of conditions for a community of people to change their idea of what and where God is, and how God is related to their daily life. Mr. Froude's inaugural lecture as professor of history at Oxford contained this paragraph: "According to Aristotle, that is the best condition of things which produces not the largest amount of knowledge or wealth, but the men of noblest nature. And I cannot see that there is any distinct progress in productions of this kind." He emphasized his words by excluding women henceforth from his lectures. How does this happen at this late date? Why, we have been preaching heaven and hell, when there is only heaven in truth; good and evil when there is only good in truth; Spirit and matter, when there is only Spirit in truth; male and female, when there is neither male nor female in Christ Jesus.

The eighth lesson explains that having deliberately made up your mind what is the idea you yourself, all alone, before truth, would best like to see demonstrated, you then take everything that happens as a help towards fulfilling your choice. I the king sends you an army to march with you, rejoice in God's signal of bounty. If the king marches an army against you, rejoice that the king fights the warrior within you when he strikes you — a warrior who was never defeated, the Spirit under whose banner you march. If you have money, God sent it. If you do not have money, sing "Rejoice, O Zion, thou shalt be redeemed without money." It is noticeable that all such as Kurozumi never take any pains to treat themselves well if they get seemingly sick; they think some miracle is being wrought through them and let the winds blow as they list.

The ninth lesson proclaims what is always known as the ninth stone of revelation, or the doctrine of cheerfulness as the breath of prosperity. Its symbol is the sunny topaz. Its practice is giving thanks and praises for the things that do indeed please you. Near you is the quickening and health-bringing Spirit. Give her thanks that she is near you, even if you do not feel her glad uplifting within your own soul. You certainly are glad that she is there near you. As you speak of how glad you are, how thankful for her presence, she will descend as breath of your breath. Give thanks that she is the life of the universe, its health, its strength, its prosperity, its protection, its skill, its love, its beauty and judgment. If it seems to you that there is not much of any of these on earth, give thanks that there even is any. Soon you will vitalize, rise up with hope, sing with expectation. Soon you will realize all you have praised here for being, Nehemiah preached this way to an immense congregation; "Neither be you sorry; for the joy of the Lord is your strength."

There is a religious sect of the Orient that practices the law of inbreathing cheerfulness after the following fashion and it makes them exceedingly strong, very healthy, very fearless: "Expel all the breath from the lungs; do this three times; then, banishing all other thoughts, let the whole heart be filled with gratitude for the blessings bestowed by Heaven. Turn the face towards the morning sun and slowly inhale the positive spirit. Hold in the breath for a short time, then turn to one side and let it slowly pass out from the lungs. When eight or nine tenths have escaped, inhale as before. The breath inhaled should be as much as possible; that exhaled should be less."

To us the process seems absurd, maybe, but being free from criticism, we soon see that it is wise to speak well of a bridge that has carried so many safely over into the upper countries of cheerful healing. It is about the same as Nehemiah's proclamation in the tenth verse to eat fat and drink wine and be exceedingly grateful. It is like our governor's yearly idea of eating the bounty of the harvests with joyful thanksgiving.

The tenth lesson explained that the mind trained to spiritual expressions finds halting places in her way, when, though she thinks nothing, she is still proceeding. If anybody has not yet learned to think nothing — nothing at all — it is a mind that has never kept the true Sabbath, even if it is a Sunday school superintendent, keeping the Sunday cessation from toil with punctiliousness.

It shows that the moment the mind is not satisfied with the fruits of its willing true thoughts it may stop thinking. As the eagle folds her wings but softly speeds onward, the mind may now rest in the Lord that He may bring it to pass.

The eleventh lesson is the history of Queen Esther, who personified the might of the Spirit in man facing awful problems of evil. As the primitive mind-cure folk of Europe would simply look at the seemingly irresistible maladies of their patients and say, "God looks you quite away", so at the look of Jesus the army fell down", and so at the look of one whose mind is set on omnipotent themes in our day also is the sin and want of a world melting into the horizons of forgotten dreams.

The twelfth lesson tells that sifting through the ethers into the hidden ears of any being forever, a voice from Jehovah keeps telling me exactly what to do. This lesson shows me that I have a faculty ready to spring into activity the instant I listen, and listen for the tones of the voice of the Motherhood of God. As the gentle mother tenderly guides the steps of her little one, so the Infinite Mother waits and fails not in her promise, "Thou shalt hear a voice behind thee saying. This is the way; walk ye in it." If I harden my will and will not be still I shall be deaf by and by. If I am deaf according to the belief of the world I may come into my hearing by silently waiting each day for the voice of the Eternal Love to be audible to my ears. This lesson also reminds its readers that people that are called deaf always insist upon doing things they do not need to do. The moments thus exercised, if spent in hearkening to every sound, though ever so slight, and through its quality detecting always a finer tone, they would soon hear all sounds. They must clear out the golden pipes of meekness in listening and persistence in the practice thereof. As light streams to the eyes upon opening their lids, so sounds stream into open ears. The spirit of light is sight. The spirit of sound is hearing. Have we not all the right to the spirit? Have we not all the right to God, who is the only Spirit?

Since the Only Spirit is in all men, is not the help of all men within them? "Is not my help in me?" cried the persecuted Job. And he proved that it was. We do not any of us need to mourn, for the spirit of joy is the breath of our breath. We do not need to be sick for the spirit of joy is our substance. Look at this closing stanza as typifying your particular troubles; sing it always:

"Ridge of mountain wave, lower thy crest!

Wail of Euroclydon, be thou at rest!

Sorrow can never be, darkness must fly,

Where saith the Light of Light,

'Peace! It is I!'"

Inter-Ocean Newspaper, March 26, 1893.

Notes

Other Books by Emma Curtis Hopkins

- *Class Lessons of 1888 (WiseWoman Press)*
- *Bible Interpretations (WiseWoman Press)*
- *Esoteric Philosophy in Spiritual Science (WiseWoman Press)*
- *Genesis Series*
- *High Mysticism (WiseWoman Press)*
- *Self Treatments with Radiant I Am (WiseWoman Press)*
- *Gospel Series (WiseWoman Press)*
- *Judgment Series in Spiritual Science (WiseWoman Press)*
- *Drops of Gold (WiseWoman Press)*
- *Resume (WiseWoman Press)*
- *Scientific Christian Mental Practice (DeVorss)*

Books about Emma Curtis Hopkins and her teachings

- *Emma Curtis Hopkins, Forgotten Founder of New Thought –* Gail Harley
- *Unveiling Your Hidden Power: Emma Curtis Hopkins' Metaphysics for the 21st Century (also as a Workbook and as A Guide for Teachers) – Ruth L. Miller*
- *Power to Heal: Easy reading biography for all ages –Ruth Miller*

To find more of Emma's work, including some previously unpublished material, log on to:

www.emmacurtishopkins.com

WISEWOMAN PRESS

1408 NE 65th St,
Vancouver, Washington 98665
800.603.3005
www.wisewomanpress.com

Books Published by WiseWoman Press

By Emma Curtis Hopkins

- *Resume*
- *The Gospel Series*
- *Class Lessons of 1888*
- *Self Treatments including Radiant I Am*
- *High Mysticism*
- *Esoteric Philosophy in Spiritual Science*
- *Drops of Gold Journal*
- *Judgment Series*
- *Bible Interpretations: Series I - XIV*

By Ruth L. Miller

- *Unveiling Your Hidden Power: Emma Curtis Hopkins' Metaphysics for the 21st Century*
- *Coming into Freedom: Emily Cady's Lessons in Truth for the 21st Century*
- *150 Years of Healing: The Founders and Science of New Thought*
- *Power Beyond Magic: Ernest Holmes Biography*
- *Power to Heal: Emma Curtis Hopkins Biography*
- *The Power of Unity: Charles Fillmore Biography*
- *The Power of Mind: Phineas P. Quimby Biography*
- *Spiritual Success*
- *Gracie's Adventures with God*
- *Uncommon Prayer*

Watch our website for release dates and order information! - www.wisewomanpress.com

List of
Bible Interpretation Series
with date from 1st to 14th Series.

This list is complete through the fourteenth Series. Emma produced at least thirty Series of Bible Interpretations.

She followed the Bible Passages provided by the International Committee of Clerics who produced the Bible Quotations for each year's use in churches all over the world.

Emma used these for her column of Bible Interpretations in both the Christian Science Magazine, at her Seminary and in the Chicago Inter-Ocean Newspaper.

First Series

Second Series

Third Series

Fourth Series

Fifth Series

Sixth Series

Seventh Series

Eighth Series

April 2 - June 25, 1893

Lesson 1	The Resurrection	April 2nd
	Matthew 28:1-10	
	One Indestructible	
	Life In Eternal Abundance	
	The Resurrection	
	Shakes Nature Herself	
	Gospel to the Poor	
Lesson 2	Universal Energy	April 9th
	Book of Job, Part 1	
Lesson 3	Strength From Confidence	April 16th
	Book of Job, Part II	
Lesson 4	The New Doctrine Brought Out	April 23rd
	Book of Job, Part III	
Lesson 5	The Golden Text	April 30th
	Proverbs 1:20-23	
	Personification Of Wisdom	
	Wisdom Never Hurts	
	The "Two" Theory	
	All is Spirit	
Lesson 6	The Law of Understanding	May 7th
	Proverbs 3	
	Shadows of Ideas	
	The Sixth Proposition	
	What Wisdom Promises	
	Clutch On Material Things	
	The Tree of Life	
	Prolonging Illuminated Moments	
Lesson 7	Self-Esteem	May 14th
	Proverbs 12:1-15	
	Solomon on Self-Esteem	
	The Magnetism of Passing Events	
	Nothing Established by Wickedness	
	Strength of a Vitalized Mind	
	Concerning the "Perverse Heart"	

111

Ninth Series

July 2 - September 27, 1893

Lesson 1	Secret of all Power	July 2nd
Acts 16: 6-15	The Ancient Chinese Doctrine of Taoism	
	Manifesting of God Powers	
	Paul, Timothy, and Silas	
	Is Fulfilling as Prophecy	
	The Inner Prompting.	
	Good Taoist Never Depressed	
Lesson 2	The Flame of Spiritual Verity	July 9th
Acts 16:18	Cause of Contention	
	Delusive Doctrines	
	Paul's History	
	Keynotes	
	Doctrine Not New	
Lesson 3	Healing Energy Gifts	July 16th
Acts 18:19-21	How Paul Healed	
	To Work Miracles	
	Paul Worked in Fear	
	Shakespeare's Idea of Loss	
	Endurance the Sign of Power	
Lesson 4	Be Still My Soul	July 23rd
Acts 17:16-24	Seeing Is Believing	
	Paul Stood Alone	
	Lessons for the Athenians	
	All Under His Power	
	Freedom of Spirit	
Lesson 5	(Missing) Acts 18:1-11	July 30th
Lesson 6	Missing No Lesson *	August 6th
Lesson 7	The Comforter is the Holy Ghost	August 13th
Acts 20	Requisite for an Orator	
	What is a Myth	
	Two Important Points	
	Truth of the Gospel	
	Kingdom of the Spirit	
	Do Not Believe in Weakness	

112

Tenth Series

October 1 – December 24, 1893

Lesson 1	*Romans 1:1-19*	October 1st
	When the Truth is Known	
	Faith in God	
	The Faithful Man is Strong	
	Glory of the Pure Motive	
Lesson 2	*Romans 3:19-26*	October 8th
	Free Grace.	
	On the Gloomy Side	
	Daniel and Elisha	
	Power from Obedience	
	Fidelity to His Name	
	He Is God	
Lesson 3	*Romans 5*	October 15th
	The Healing Principle	
	Knows No Defeat.	
	In Glorified Realms	
	He Will Come	
Lesson 4	*Romans 12:1*	October 22nd
	Would Become Free	
	Man's Co-operation	
	Be Not Overcome	
	Sacrifice No Burden	
	Knows the Future	
Lesson 5	*I Corinthians 8:1-13*	October 29th
	The Estate of Man	
	Nothing In Self	
	What Paul Believed	
	Doctrine of Kurozumi	
Lesson 6	*I Corinthians 12:1-26*	November 5th
	Science of The Christ Principle	
	Dead from the Beginning	
	St. Paul's Great Mission	
	What The Spark Becomes	
	Chris, All There Is of Man	
	Divinity Manifest in Man	
	Christ Principle Omnipotent	

114

Eleventh Series

January 1 – March 25, 1894

Lesson 1	*Genesis 1:26-31 & 2:1-3*	January 7th
	The First Adam	
	Man: The Image of Language Paul and Elymas	
Lesson 2	*Genesis 3:1-15*	January 14th
	Adam's Sin and God's Grace	
	The Fable of the Garden	
	Looked-for Sympathy	
	The True Doctrine	
Lesson 3	*Genesis 4:3-13*	January 21st
	Types of the Race	
	God in the Murderer	
	God Nature Unalterable	
Lesson 4	*Genesis 9:8-17*	January 28th
	God's Covenant With Noah	
	Value of Instantaneous Action	
	The Lesson of the Rainbow	
Lesson 5	I Corinthians 8:1-13	February 4th
	Genesis 12:1-9	
	Beginning of the Hebrew Nation	
	No Use For Other Themes	
	Influence of Noble Themes	
	Danger In Looking Back	
Lesson 6	*Genesis 17:1-9*	February 11th
	God's Covenant With Abram	
	As Little Children	
	God and Mammon	
	Being Honest With Self	
Lesson 7	*Genesis 18:22-23*	February 18th
	God's Judgment of Sodom	
	No Right Nor Wrong In Truth	
	Misery Shall Cease	
Lesson 8	*Genesis 22:1-13*	February 25th
	Trial of Abraham's Faith	
	Light Comes With Preaching	
	You Can Be Happy NOW	

117

Twelfth Series

April 1 – June 24, 1894

119

Thirteenth Series

July 1 – September 30, 1894

Lesson 1 The Birth of Jesus   July 1st
Luke 2:1-16
No Room for Jesus
Man's Mystic Center
They glorify their Performances

Lesson 2 Presentation in the Temple July 8th
Luke 2:25-38
A Light for Every Man
All Things Are Revealed
The Coming Power
Like the Noonday Sun

Lesson 3 Visit of the Wise Men   July 15th
Matthew 1:2-12
The Law Our Teacher
Take neither Scrip nor Purse
The Star in the East
The Influence of Truth

Lesson 4 Flight Into Egypt   July 22nd
Mathew 2:13-23
The Magic Word of Wage Earning
How Knowledge Affect the Times
The Awakening of the Common People

Lesson 5 The Youth of Jesus   July 29th
Luke2:40-52
Your Righteousness is as filthy Rags
Whatsoever Ye Search, that will Ye Find
The starting Point of All Men
Equal Division, the Lesson Taught by Jesus
The True Heart Never Falters

Lesson 6 The "All is God" Doctrine August 5th
Luke 2:40-52
Three Designated Stages of Spiritual Science
Christ Alone Gives Freedom
The Great Leaders of Strikes

Lesson 7 Missing   August 12th
Lesson 8 First Disciples of Jesus August 19th
John 1:36-49
The Meaning of Repentance

120

Fourteenth Series

9077709R0

Made in the USA
Charleston, SC
09 August 2011